"*Why Would Anyone Go to Chu*[...] a place, and a people. Ultimately [...] incarnation of the gospel. Read t[...] [...] wnat the world needs now is incarnation. Read it and discover all over again what is so compelling about not just going to church but being the church."

David Fitch, author of *Faithful Presence* and
professor at Northern Seminary, Chicago

"My generation is searching for things we've lost: a sense of community, a sense of the sacred, healthier lifestyles, and places where our best values and ideas are encouraged and practiced. Kevin does the hard work—intellectually and practically—of championing church as a potential resolution to these searches. And as the title suggests, *Why Would Anyone Go to Church?* doesn't avoid any of the hard questions this proposition raises. Best of all, it is not theoretical; this book is the story of ordinary people in Hamilton, Ontario, doing something wonderfully old and new at the same time."

Shad (Shadrach Kabango), artist and
host of Netflix's *Hip-Hop Evolution*

"Right from the beginning, this book doesn't shy away from the frightening questions being asked about what is happening to church and whether there is any hope for it. Because of this, I knew I could trust Kevin as he led me through his difficult and joyful journey of pastoring a church. I thoroughly enjoyed *Why Would Anyone Go to Church?* not just for its great storytelling and insightful practices but because of the revelation that those involved in participating in the church are not the ones who win or lose but the ones who are irrevocably transformed."

Scott Erickson, artist and coauthor of
Prayer and *May It Be So*

"*Why Would Anyone Go to Church?* inspires people to experience and express the beauty and brokenness of life in the local church. Thank you, Kevin, for helping the Good News message shine more brightly as we join together in true community in the places where Jesus has put us."

Bruxy Cavey, teaching pastor at The Meeting House and author of *The End of Religion* and *(re)union*

"*Why Would Anyone Go to Church?* is a spiritual memoir of millennial church planting in a post-Christian world. Makins's love for his city and his neighborhood shines brilliantly through this exploration of failure, community, and loving the universal by focusing on the particular—in this case, the local church."

D. L. Mayfield, writer and neighbor

"I can think of no other subgenre of literature more preferable to avoid than memoirs from faith leaders and first-person accounts of their own faith communities—inevitably more hagiography than biography, real stories are flattened in the process of making saints and manufacturing meaning. And then along comes this surprising, astonishing gem of a book. I love Kevin Makins's *Why Would Anyone Go to Church?* for its unvarnished, unflinching honesty; incisive, beautiful writing; authentic belly laughs; and for the many moments I had to put it down, gut-punched by the sheer holiness and humanity in these pages. It made me fall in love with the church again, despite myself. This startling book on Christian community is too unlike anything else to be the one you came looking for but, if you're like me, precisely the one your soul has craved. Bonhoeffer gave us *Life Together*; Kevin Makins has given us a less reverent, more complex, more human story of what life together looks like here and now."

Jonathan Martin, author of *How to Survive a Shipwreck* and *Prototype*

WHY WOULD ANYONE GO TO CHURCH?

WHY WOULD ANYONE GO TO CHURCH?

A Young Community's Quest
to Reclaim Church for Good

KEVIN MAKINS

BakerBooks

a division of Baker Publishing Group
Grand Rapids, Michigan

Published by Baker Books
a division of Baker Publishing Group
PO Box 6287, Grand Rapids, MI 49516-6287
www.bakerbooks.com

Printed in the United States of America

Library of Congress Cataloging-in-Publication Data
Names: Makins, Kevin, 1986– author.
Title: Why would anyone go to church? : a young community's quest to reclaim church for good / Kevin Makins.
Description: Grand Rapids, Michigan : Baker Books, a division of Baker Publishing Group, 2020. | Includes bibliographical references.
Identifiers: LCCN 2019055544 | ISBN 9781540900005 (paperback)
Subjects: LCSH: Church development, New. | Church. | Eucharist Church (Hamilton, Ont.) | Hamilton (Ont.)—Church history.
Classification: LCC BV652.24 .M345 2020 | DDC 253—dc23
LC record available at https://lccn.loc.gov/2019055544

Some names and details have been changed to protect the privacy of the individuals involved.

The author is represented by the literary agency of Credo Communications, LLC, www.credocommunications.net.

20 21 22 23 24 25 26   7 6 5 4 3 2 1

To my wife, my mother,
and that guy who recognized me on a writing
retreat at the monastery and spent twenty minutes
telling me how much our church had let him down.

You kept this book humble.

CONTENTS

PROLOGUE

Why Would Anyone Do This?

Two summers ago, my wife decided she wanted to be a DJ. The challenge was that she only wanted to play *emo*, short for *emotional music*, a subgenre that rose in popularity during the early 2000s when millennials like us were going through our most over-the-top heartbreak. One popular lyric from the time, undoubtedly tattooed on hundreds of thirtysomething moms today, reads, "The truth is you could slit my throat, and . . . I'd apologize for bleeding on your shirt."

You can see why this stuff isn't in regular clubbing rotations.

My wife knew the only way she could DJ a full set of emo hits would be to throw the party herself, so she rented out a local bar, printed off hundreds of posters, and decorated the entire venue, including a MySpace selfie booth in the back. Our friends arrived first, donning old band T-shirts and wearing studded belts, but an hour later, the place was packed with total strangers: punk rockers with big, spiky hair, college students with caked-on black eyeliner, hipsters on cocaine, grungy anarchists, and parents who had finally gotten their kids to bed and were ready to relive their youth. Sad anthems blasted through the speakers as heavy boots and Converse shoes jumped to the beat, the old wooden floors vibrating beneath us.

Then I noticed a guy who was definitely having a little too much fun. He was tall and had a round face with bloodshot, dopey eyes. I knew Dopey Eyes. He had visited our church on a couple of occasions over the past few months, and while pastors are supposed to be agents of grace and compassion, the truth is, I always found him a little grating. But that's when he was sober. Tonight he was on a whole other level, trying to sing along but mostly just yelling in people's faces, trying to jump around but mostly knocking people over.

There was shouting behind me, and I turned to see an angry giant pushing his way through the crowd. He had a shaved head, a thick, dark beard, and a beet-red face from fury or drugs—or both. He also had a single rage vein running up the side of his neck and looping over his bald head. He stormed into the middle of the party and shoved Dopey Eyes hard in the chest, knocking him to the ground. Rage Vein leaned down, and sweat dripped onto his victim's frightened round face: "I'm only gonna tell you once. Get out of here, or you'll regret it!" The music continued to play, but no one was dancing; everyone was just staring at the two of them. Dopey Eyes slowly rose to his feet and shuffled his way to the exit. Hoping to avoid any more drama, I left for a toilet break.

As I walked down the bar's skinny hallway, the sound of rock-and-roll heartbreak grew muffled behind me. At 1:30 a.m., the bathroom was not looking so hot. The dark red walls were tagged from top to bottom in black marker—mostly with phone numbers and phallic imagery. Toilet paper had fallen to the floor and rolled open, the sink was running for no one, and the ground was soaked with what I hoped was tap water or beer. I slid into the stall and attempted to relieve myself, when I heard the door to the bathroom being kicked open. It hit the wall with a SLAM. Someone stormed in, shouting profanities before full-swing punching my stall, which shook violently. I jumped against the far wall and froze. I could see movement through the crack of the door. Slowly, carefully, I peeked out from the stall to see what was going on. It was Rage Vein and three of his friends. He was pacing back and forth across the room. "I'm going to knock him out!" he shouted at the ceiling, bouncing around the tiny bathroom in a hurricane of fury.

I cautiously stepped into the open and approached Rage Vein carefully, as if de-escalating a grizzly. "Is . . . is this about the kid you pushed?" I asked, trying not to make any sudden movements.

"What?" he spit out as he noticed me for the first time. "Yeah. That kid was yelling at everyone, then he bodychecked my friends and spilled my girl's drink all over her. So now I'm gonna drag him outside and knock him out."

"No! No, no. Hold on." I stumbled forward, hands held out. "You don't have to do that."

"He's asking for it."

"Oh, I'm sure he is," I responded. "I know that kid and I agree he's being super annoying . . . but I can't let you beat him up."

"Why not?" he snapped back.

"Because . . ." there was a brief pause as I looked to the ground, sighed, and finally admitted, "because . . . I'm his pastor."

This, for the record, is exactly what I don't like about church. The fact is, I found this kid irritating from the moment I met him, and seeing him sloppy drunk made me like him even less. This wasn't the kind of person I wanted associated with our church. He was the last person I would have picked to join my team. It was so tempting to sneak out of the bathroom and remain uninvolved.

But I tell you this story because, for some reason, this guy had decided to walk into our church service two or three times prior to this dance party, and that small action meant that, in some inconvenient and infuriating way, I was now connected to him. I couldn't let him get jumped outside the bar, even if a swift punch in the head might have been good for him.

In seminary, I learned how to preach sermons and study the Bible. I was taught how to plan Sunday services and make hospital visits.

But being associated with people I wouldn't have chosen and don't particularly like? That was an element of church I didn't see coming.

Then again, there were a lot of things about church I didn't see coming. I didn't expect to start a community full of spiritual misfits when I was just twenty-three years old. I didn't know how much fun it would be to make up our own holy days or how vital a good sense of humor would be. I didn't realize how much pushback we'd get from more established religious organizations or the myriad ways people in our own congregation would hurt and disappoint each other.

Perhaps most unexpected was when my wife and I attended a church planting assessment center, the tried-and-true way to know if God has called you to start a new Christian community. After three days of grueling psychological and spiritual warfare, the experts flunked us and said, "God has not called you to church plant, and to do so would put your community and your own souls in jeopardy." This was awkward news to receive, especially since we had started our church years earlier.

I'll get to these stories in a little while, but I mention them now to let you know what you're getting into. This book is unflinchingly honest and often humiliating. When we set out to start a new congregation, it was because we had a desire to connect with people that "organized religion" seemed to miss. We had more questions than answers, questions that couldn't be solved by reading another book or attending more lectures. We had to live out the answers together, little by little, over a long period of time. We had to get our hands dirty.

But that's not such a bad thing. I've always found God most present in the mess.

Totally Outclassed

Dramatic bar fights aside, most people in our church are pretty easy to love. Today, our community is made up of college students and seasoned saints, lots of young adults and a seemingly never-ending onslaught of squishy babies. There are artists and doctors, baristas and software engineers, stay-at-home parents and the occasionally employed. There are cyclists and advocates and porch sitters. Together we've created a home for skeptics who had never warmed a pew bench and for religious burnouts who ran away years ago. Perhaps the best description I've heard of our church is that we are a "front door/back door" community. Many in our congregation are either entirely new to faith, coming in through the front door, or they are people who grew disenchanted with the traditional church, but on their way out the back door, a friend suggested they give it one more try with us. These two groups couldn't be more different. They've had entirely opposite experiences, but they find themselves crossing paths in the same place: the edge of faith, on the borderland between the sacred and secular, the profound and profane. Together they are asking the most pressing questions:

> "What does Christian community look like for this next generation?"
>
> "Who will it be for?"
>
> And the big one: "Why would anyone go to church?"

My assumption is that for many of you reading this, the word *church* immediately raises some red flags. Many of us picture Christians rallying behind politicians and theological camps, engaged in a never-ending culture war. We think about all the times we've seen congregations fixated on growth and success, buying bigger buildings with larger parking lots and the occasional private jet. We've heard preachers justify racism and bigotry with smooth spiritual language. Christians online often seem hypocritical, fearful, and self-righteous. Organized religion has covered up sexual abuse scandals and participated in cultural genocide. Christian communities have often functioned as a judgmental courtroom instead of a loving home.

For all these reasons and more, church isn't exactly popular these days. Most of my nonreligious neighbors assume that every congregation is full of closed-minded bigots, but even Christians I know are wondering whether church is a necessary component of faith. CNN reports that statistically about half of all the young people raised in American churches will walk away disillusioned. The Canadian Broadcasting Corporation has said that my country is on track to close over nine thousand sacred buildings in the next decade, roughly one-third of all our religious spaces.

Maybe the church has just been outclassed in the modern world. Local music venues will host better concerts, while comedy clubs and storytelling events give you more thoughtful and honest reflection. Yoga nurtures a sense of spiritual calm, and any club or team can connect you with like-minded people. And that's before you consider all the internet has given us: TED talks and podcasts feature the world's best communicators, streaming services allow every piece of music to be just one click away, and social media pulls from hundreds of millions of people to find others who think just like you. And it's all so instant. Forget waiting until Sunday; in your pocket right now is every song and lecture, every documentary and article you could ever ask for.

What does the church offer us that can compete with all that?

To start, churches usually meet on Sunday morning, one of the two days of the week most of us are allowed to sleep in. They have eager greeters with clammy hands. The sanctuary is always too hot or too cold but never just right. Typically the music is either an organ, the most expensive and unruly instrument in all of human history, or a bunch of dads shredding guitar solos to the added chorus of "Be Thou My Vision." There is reciting of old prayers and a surprising amount of standing and sitting, followed up by a book report on a two-thousand-year-old letter written to a tiny community in a backwater city of the ancient world. Then everyone heads to the fellowship hall to make small talk over mediocre coffee.

People give up free evenings to go to Bible study and catechism classes. They join teams and committees. They budget for the church, clean the carpets, and run Friday night youth group for teenagers who haven't yet discovered deodorant.

And do they get paid to make all this happen? No. They *give* money to be a part of it. Many people give *ten percent of their income* for the honor of doing all this weird religious stuff.

People ask me if I'm surprised that so many are leaving the church. Surprised? Are you kidding me? I can't believe *anyone* still does this church thing. And yet they do. For two thousand years, people have continued to be a part of the church, despite war and persecution and corruption and organ music.

Why has church survived? Surely something has made it so meaningful to so many people for such a long period of time.

That's what we were trying to understand when we started a new church a decade ago. What we discovered is that few of our peers are interested in competing with the culture around us. The Jesus followers I know aren't sticking with the church because church is better than a concert or more interesting than a podcast. They're staying because there are primordial elements of Christian community that are far more rooted than all that superficial fluff.

These are the deeper truths that need to be uncovered if this next generation is going to reclaim church for good.

Each chapter of this book will explore one of these truths we've learned about church, while sharing both my story and our congregation's journey. I should point out that I have no special authority when it comes to this stuff. All I have is our testimony, which I have tried to share honestly while also being as charitable as possible. Every event described is my own best recollection, which is fallible to memory and bias; though, as you'll see, I don't always come out unscathed. While I have occasionally played with the sequence of events, everything is true as best as I can capture it.

Word Made Flesh

If we're setting the table for the rest of this book, allow me to make one final arrangement before we sit down.

At the center of the Christian faith is the story of incarnation: God becoming human in the person of Jesus. Or, as the author of the Gospel of John puts it, "The Word became flesh." When I look around the modern world, I see a lot of opinions. Every day my Twitter feed is filled with thoughts, rants, and think pieces about how things should be. We have no shortage of words. But the church presents us with a challenging question: Can you make that word . . . flesh?

Can you put it into practice? With thirty people? With a hundred people? With two thousand people? Can you take that abstract idea and live it out together? And if you can't . . . no offense, but I'm just not interested. There are enough opinions out there. We've got plenty of words. We need more flesh.

We need incarnation.

Over the years we've come to see the church as an incarnational force. Perhaps it's fitting that, historically and biblically, the church has been referred to in feminine language, both as the bride of Christ and as our mother. The church isn't an *it* at all. The church is a *she*. And she refused to let us stand at a distance.

Church threw us into adventure and difficult relationships. She called us to redeem our city streets and our calendar. She taught us how to seek unity in our differences, how to forgive those who hurt us, and how to process rejection. More than anything, she refused to let our ideas stay in our heads. When we said, "Christians should feed the world," she responded, "Great, there's a refugee family down the street and they need a meal." When we cheered, "Christians should love everyone," she replied, "Good, now go spend time with this one annoying person."

Which brings me back to an emo dance party filled with sad boys and girls.

After narrowly avoiding a bloodbath, I dragged a very intoxicated Dopey Eyes out onto the snow-covered sidewalk and called him a cab. While we waited, I launched into a stern pastoral lecture about how he was acting, and then, out of nowhere, he started to cry. I was so angry with him for being a numbskull and annoyed that, instead of dancing at my wife's party, I was stuck babysitting a twenty-year-old in the frigid cold. And yet, at the same time, I felt strangely grateful. Grateful that the church was inviting me to make the word flesh—not on a scenic hike or in a beautiful cathedral but outside a dingy bar on a winter night.

Despite my reservations, I stepped forward and hugged Dopey Eyes. His tears began to fall and soak the shoulder of my jacket. I shook my head and thought:

So this is church . . .

Why would anyone do this?

1 GETTING OUR HANDS DIRTY

No one comes to Jesus without first encountering the church.

Sometimes the connection is obvious. Many of you reading this book were raised as faithful Sunday attendees or joined up after a friend invited you to a weekly Bible study. Other times, the connection to church is more subtle. If you prayed in a moment of desperation, it's because someone (a friend, a grandparent, or even that weirdo on the Christian radio station) taught you that there was such a thing as prayer and that it was a real way to speak to God. If a book helped you understand faith in a new way, you have to recognize that the author was writing out of their own history with church. Even if you first heard about Jesus when you were all alone, flipping through a Bible while bored on a work trip, it's only because a bunch of Gideons snuck into the hotel room first and hid it for you to discover. And they also are a part of the church.

I don't know how you would describe your beliefs. You may be someone who would comfortably use the label

"Christian," or perhaps you'd prefer to check the "no" or "it's complicated" box. What I know for sure is that you didn't arrive there in isolation. When it comes to faith, we're all growing out of the same soil. Whether our experience has been positive or negative, we can't talk about Jesus without talking about church. And that requires looking back.

Pilgrim

What is your first memory of church?

As a kid, I thought I attended the only church in the world. Even back then, the Canadian culture was thoroughly secular. My classmates didn't talk about Jesus, and my neighbors' cars sat in their driveways on Sunday mornings. While my friends were at home playing Super Nintendo, I was putting on a white button-up shirt, tan corduroys, and cheap black dress shoes that, if you kicked at just the right angle, would leave a long, black streak on the floor of Pilgrim Lutheran Church. My early church memories are of a wonderfully ordinary community. One-hour gatherings ran through the same words, repeated week after week, the cadence and chants now lovingly carved like initials into the tree bark of my mind. "Lamb of God, who takes away the sins of the world, have mercy upon us."

The congregation numbered no more than ninety on a given Sunday, but each person had a role to play. The parents washed dishes after coffee hour, seniors babysat the children and tithed, young adults flirted, and we kids sat silently in the back rows, playing with tiny trucks and chewing on Cheerios next to a sign that proudly declared: "These Pews Reserved for Parents of Small Children."

Our denomination was Lutheran, but Pastor Schnarr was quick to point out we were "Lutheran Church—Missouri Synod," the more conservative of the two streams, which had emerged after a messy split in 1963. These party lines ran not only through our congregation but through our extended family as well. Pastor Schnarr was also my uncle, and his siblings were split on which brand of Lutheranism deserved our loyalty.

Theological knowledge was highly valued in our church. By the time I was nine, I was expected not only to sit silently through the service but also to be in the front row, listening at full attention. Every week Pastor Schnarr would give the kids a quiz sheet, which had questions about the sermon written on it:

"Why do we love God?"

"How do we know our faith is true?"

"What do we do to earn salvation?"

I absolutely destroyed these quizzes, nailing the answers with extreme Lutheran focus:

"We love God because God first loved us."

"The Bible is God's Word to us and fully trustworthy for all matters of faith, life, and doctrine."

"Nothing; salvation is the free gift of God, given to dead sinners."

You might think I was a model theologian, eager to expand my knowledge of the Lord, but the real reason was far more childish: if we answered correctly, Pastor Schnarr gave us a full-size candy bar.

Half of my theological education was motivated by that chocolate.

Seeds

After two years of weekly classes, I was officially "confirmed" in the Lutheran church and invited forward for Communion. This part of the service, often called "the Lord's Supper" or "the

Eucharist," is when the congregation comes forward to a table where they receive a bit of bread and wine, which represents Jesus's last meal with his disciples. Standing with me were a few thirteen-year-old peers, who had also spent over a hundred Thursday afternoons in the church hall with Pastor Schnarr, learning the foundation of Christian theology (Jesus is Lord) and Lutheranism (Luther was also pretty great). In an ironic twist, this ended up being one of the last times we all came to the table together. Once their children were confirmed in the faith and officially committed to following Jesus, parents seemed a great deal more lax about their kids' Sunday attendance. At first, just a few of the youth dropped off due to hockey practice. Then, others had piano lessons. One after another, the youth of Pilgrim vanished until my sister, my cousins, and I were all that remained. The pew in the back row, the one reserved "For Parents of Small Children," now sat empty most weeks. The Lutheran church was becoming a statistic, experiencing radical decline like so many other North American congregations. At the time, I wasn't too troubled; while I was fine to sit in a pew once a week, it was mostly because my parents made me go. My personal connection to church—and to faith—was still quite shallow.

Some seeds lie dormant a long time before they begin to grow.

Gardener

The Bible often uses images of gardening to describe God's work in the world. Jesus talks about the Good News being like seeds that are scattered. Some land on the gravel and are eaten by birds; other seeds shoot up quickly but die just as fast. Thankfully, some seeds find a home in the dirt and begin to crack open. Over time they will sprout, stretch up, and produce fruit and even more seeds. Jesus also describes a farmer who goes to sleep and awakens to see that the crops have been growing, even while he did nothing. Jesus asks his listeners to consider the mustard seed, which is small and seemingly insignificant and yet becomes a massive plant, tearing through dirt and creating a home for the birds of the air. The apostle Paul, one of the earliest church leaders, describes the life of a congregation in agricultural terms, noting that while he planted seeds and others watered, only God could make it grow.

And then there is Mary Magdalene, who encountered the resurrected Jesus and mistook him for a gardener.

And she was correct.

The resurrected Jesus is the great Gardener, cultivating a new creation in the midst of the old. The new creation breaks through the hardened soil, gives shelter to those toiling under the sun, and nourishes the world through all that it yields.

What a compelling image! Who wouldn't want to be part of that movement?

Except, the Bible tells us the tangible expression of this new creation is . . . the church?

I remember being sixteen and looking around our sanctuary, seeing gray hair and decade-old felt banners, and thinking, "This is God's plan to save the world?" I was bored by the church and distracted by other, more important things. Like sports and friends and video games and *girls*.

But Jesus is sneaky.

Girls

My friend and I were hanging out on the beach when we saw them: cuties. It was the summer before our last year of high school, and we were desperate for female attention. We stood around them awkwardly until they finally said hello. The three of them were sisters. There was the blonde-haired punk rocker; the brunette, who was sweet as sugar; and the one I was smitten with, the spunky redhead.

As summer vacation came to a close, I discovered a secret that scrambled my teenage brain: the cuties were Christians. The Lutheran church I went to was a closed loop; we didn't have summer camps or youth conferences. Up to this point, I had assumed that my sister, my cousins, and I were the only remaining young Christians in the world. I felt blindsided. Luckily, I had a secret weapon with which to impress the ladies: my thorough religious education. I attempted to bond with them over Luther's forty-first thesis, but it was completely ineffective. Turns out they were some other breed of Christian that I had no category for at the time: charismatic Christians. These are the shout-it-out, *on fire*, "PRAISE JEEEE-SUS!" zealots you picture when you imagine a tent revival. They were into the baptism of the Holy Spirit, hour-long worship sessions, and knowing your spiritual gifts. I thought they were lazy theologians.

That fall, the blonde and brunette sisters kept inviting me to their youth group, another part of their foreign religious culture I didn't understand. Lutherans didn't have youth group. We had catechism. I gave them a "no" and listed off a bunch of good reasons I would never give up my Friday night to hang out in some Bible chapel.

Then the third sister, the one I had a crush on, asked me if I'd like to go. "I'd go to hell for you," I replied. "How bad can youth group be?"

Enter the other half of my theological motivation—girls.

Germination

Looking back on those times can be very confusing. Most youth groups are a tangled web of holiness and hormones, grace and circle games. They are politically incorrect sermon illustrations, road trips without enough seat belts, and awkward "sex talk" nights. Youth groups are often bad theology with good intentions, a handful of burned-out volunteers, and a bunch of needy kids. I can't separate out what is good from what is bad or what is helpful from what is harmful. It's a cocktail: once it's shaken together, your only options are to dump it or drink it.

Nevertheless, for me, youth group was incredibly helpful. I learned how to pray out loud with friends, how to share my faith with other people in a way that was authentic, and how to worship God without an organ. More than anything else, I experienced Christian community, seeing firsthand what it looked like as a teenager to love God. The youth group was almost entirely youth led, which meant we were quickly given responsibilities and often made mistakes, but it didn't matter. We were a part of something bigger than ourselves. We had a mission, which gave a direction for our teenage angst. We experienced rapid growth that year. I'm still not quite sure how to make sense of it. When I joined in the fall, the youth group was made up of about thirty people, but by the end of the school year, over a hundred teens were showing up every Friday night. Many hadn't grown up in church, but we were all learning how to love God and each other while eating our way through the youth budget.

Even as teens decided to follow Jesus, none of us really knew how church fit into the equation. As far as we could tell, entering into a personal relationship with God was what really mattered; then we could decide whether to tack on going to church.

The most rapid spiritual growth of my life happened during that last year of high school. In my naïveté, all I saw were the green shoots that were suddenly breaking through the surface.

I forgot that each one of them had come from an old seed, which had been patiently sown over a lifetime.

Rebaptized

Shortly after my youth group revival, I was baptized . . . again. As a newborn, water had been poured onto my head, sealing me with the promises of God within the community of his people. But my nineteen-year-old brain was only excited by what had happened in the last year and needed some way to express it. Despite being long-standing Lutherans, my parents respected my wishes and even came to the baptism ceremony to show support. We weren't in a sanctuary this time but at a small lake just outside the city. I went up to the microphone to share my testimony and gave an impassioned speech about the youth group, explaining that now I was *finally* able to understand what it meant to be a Christian. Everyone in the crowd cheered, and I went under the water full of holy fire. When I emerged, I looked out at the smiling faces and immediately felt doused and confused. My mom was clapping along in support, but her red eyes and sullen face revealed something was off.

After the baptism, I found her sitting at the edge of the lake, staring over the water. She didn't want to talk about her running mascara, but I pestered her until she opened up. "I'm so glad that you love God and want to follow Jesus, and I'm grateful for your youth group," she said to me through tears, "but you sort of threw the Lutheran church under the bus. You talked about us like we were part of the problem, as if God hadn't done anything in your life before now. But I remember all the Sunday school teachers who invested in you and how Pastor Schnarr would sit in the office and quiz you on the Bible, and the hundreds of times you and I had honest conversations about faith when you were a kid. You forgot all of that." I felt punched in the gut. She was right.

In the process of making my faith my own, I had failed to recognize all I had received.

Nurtured and Wounded

Maybe you can relate to that feeling. You look back on the church you were raised in or the youth group you were a part of and feel a coldness or resentment. You don't believe what you believed back then. You don't see things the way you used to. Ironically, just a few years after my baptism, I'd come to feel quite cynical about my years in the youth group as well. It's tempting to dismiss what we've recently moved on from.

But part of growing up is recognizing how we arrived at the place where we are. It's a long process, but we're always a product of where we've been planted, at the mercy of those who came before us.

Some of you had a negative experience of church. Perhaps that was the place where you first learned who was *not* welcome or which political party was God's favorite. Maybe church was where you were judged for how you dressed or where you were taught not to ask hard questions. Tragically, some people reading this were taught that God is angry, always on the edge of throwing you into hell, simply because you have doubts or are a thirteen-year-old boy who is attracted to other boys.

But there are other stories. Perhaps church was the place where you experienced unconditional love, learned to play an instrument, or had someone older than you invest in your life for the first time. The church taught many of us to forgive, to be patient, and to trust God when we feel that we are in over our heads. The church tied us into a long story filled with saints and sinners, giant fish and fiery furnaces, death and resurrection. She gave us a narrative out of which we could live our lives.

At the very least, the church taught me how to be bored for an hour. That builds character.

I don't want to downplay the harm that church has done. Nor do I want to ignore all the good. The truth is that most of us have experienced a bit of both. Church is a family, and I don't know anyone who wasn't simultaneously nurtured and wounded by their parents.

But we cannot ignore the more extreme situations. Many of us know someone who was sinned against by someone in the church in a way that can only be described as evil. If you're reading this and you experienced abuse by those in the church who were supposed to nurture you, I do not know what to say except that I am so sorry. I am so, so sorry that happened to you, and I believe Jesus is with you and weeps with you. I hope that through good counseling, prayer, and relationships, you will be able to find deep healing and that, in time, God will use your story to encourage, build up, and protect others. The master Gardener is really good at taking the crap of our lives and turning it into fertilizer.

That said, it's important for us to remember that in most cases, the church is made up of simple people trying their best to help. They didn't intend to cause any harm. They were just dumb.

You know, like the rest of us.

Perhaps when your parents didn't see the growth they wanted, they accidentally overwatered the garden, drowning out the small sprouts. Maybe your youth leader trampled around the mud in his big, heavy boots, and instead of helping, he flattened the tiny bud that was blooming. We don't need to excuse such ignorance or pretend it wasn't hurtful. But we can be mature enough to forgive those who, with the best of intentions, accidentally harmed us. They were products of their environment just as we are products of ours. We can give them grace, knowing that while we are no better than they are, we must learn from their successes and mistakes. We must continue to grow.

Throughout this book, I'm going to share more than a couple of strong opinions about church, but I hope by now you recognize that this isn't just to fling mud at those who came before us. Rather, we honor those who have gone before us by going further than they could. Someday, my daughter is going to point the finger at me and my fifty-year-old friends and tell us that we never should have been driving cars, eating avocado toast, listening to hip-hop music, or . . . I don't know what. That's precisely the point. She'll see things we missed and go further than we can *because* she's standing on our shoulders. Even Jesus said that his disciples would do greater things than he had done.

That's how this movement was always meant to work.

Hands-On

When I was five years old, my Sunday school teacher, Mrs. Francis, told my parents that I asked good questions and was going to be a pastor. The older I got, the more this prophecy haunted me, staring down at me like the Eye of Sauron. I ran for cover. Why would I commit to a dying organization all my friends thought was irrelevant? Who volunteers to work on the Titanic?

You may not have had this exact experience, but I imagine many of you have asked the same questions I did: Why church? Why stick around? Why should I get on my knees and work in the soil?

These are big questions that you and God need to wrestle through together. But perhaps I can simply invite you to consider the ways you've already gotten a little dirt under your fingernails. Where has God placed you and with whom? How are you already pulling up weeds, handling prickly thorns with extra care, or watering the tiny sprouts around you?

If you're a follower of Jesus, then your faith bloomed in a particular garden. Who cultivated the plot in which you grew? What does it look like for you to learn from their wisdom and their mistakes? What could it practically look like for you to take things further than those who came before you?

How can you get your hands dirty?

Mrs. Francis's seeds lay dormant despite my youth group revival. My commitment to follow Jesus was a prayer that ended with ". . . but I won't become a pastor." Despite my protest, over the years, I began to see that I had a role to play in the church and that perhaps it was more hands-on than I had anticipated. It was only after dropping out of college, working a string of bad jobs, and eventually being fired from the night shift at a fast-food restaurant that I was humble enough to start working in the manure.

I had no idea how messy things would get.

2 FALLING INTO PLACE

The story of our church can't be separated from the story of Hamilton, Ontario. The story of Hamilton can't be separated from the story of steel. And in the 1950s, the steel industry in Hamilton was booming.

On the northern edge of my city is Lake Ontario, one of the five Great Lakes, which together make up the largest freshwater source on Earth. Ambitious entrepreneurs quickly realized this could be exploited (and polluted) by dropping factories along the shoreline. These factories also created immense job opportunities. At its peak in the 1980s, nearly thirty thousand citizens were employed by the largest steel mill in the city. But as the demand for Canadian steel cooled, tens of thousands of people lost their jobs. The public infrastructure also took a blow. Large one-way streets, designed to move thousands of cars in and out of busy factories, were now radically underused, creating four-lane concrete deserts in the middle of historic neighborhoods. Businesses shut down, leaving storefront displays frozen in time, vestiges of a once vibrant neighborhood. Many of the men who lost their jobs had spent decades working in the factories, assuming they were safe until retirement. Instead, they were spit out early into a world that had moved on. Finding meaningful work proved challenging, and this led to unemployment, addiction, an increase in violent crime, and undiagnosed mental health challenges. All of this created a spiral of poverty. As the infrastructure deteriorated, apartments became cheaper and more people of little means moved to the city. There are even stories of other nearby cities shipping their poor citizens to Hamilton.

But this was only half of the story. The economic struggle of Hamilton was caged in. The southern edge of downtown runs into an escarpment—a glacier-carved wall that stretches west across the entire inner city and east all the way to Niagara Falls. It's 328 vertical feet of green trees, waterfalls, old beer cans, and used condoms. Resting on top of this escarpment, referred to unironically as "the mountain," is the other half of Hamilton. On the mountain, you had suburbs and strip malls, two-car garages and chain stores, newly constructed neighborhoods and a private high school. There was opportunity, investment, and a general attitude of superiority.

That was me. I was raised on the mountain, literally *above* the problems of downtown. My friends and I were pretty judgmental and dismissive about whatever was going on "down there." That is, until my eleventh-grade summer job included a daily bus commute down the escarpment and into the chaos of Beasley Park, which at the time was the third-poorest neighborhood in Canada.

Beasley Park

My supervisor greeted me on my first day as a camp counselor and gave me a tour of the park. She explained that our summer camp would involve thirty kids from the neighborhood, many of whom didn't yet speak English. She pointed out some stumps at the edge of the park; the trees had recently been cut down to stop pedophiles from hiding in them and masturbating. Then she explained that the water fountain had to be turned off because too many homeless people had been bathing in it. Later that day I walked out the back door of the community center and found two men heating up heroin on a spoon. I shuffled back down the hall to my twenty-eight-year-old supervisor's office and mentioned it to her. Calmly and clinically, she kicked the back door open and yelled: "*What the hell are you doing? There are kids in here! Get out!*"

It was overwhelming. It was terrifying.

And I loved it.

I was fascinated by the way the kids cared for each other. One of the camp leaders told me about a five-year-old girl who lived with her bedridden grandmother and how two nine-year-olds walked to her apartment to pick her up for school every morning. They would bring her to our community center to make sure she ate breakfast before they dropped her off at kindergarten. After school, the nine-year-olds walked the girl to their house for dinner. Finally, they would take her home to her grandma's and make sure she brushed her teeth before bed. The next morning, they'd be back to pick her up. They did this every day.

This five-year-old and I bonded. She had a giant toothy smile and an infectious laugh. When I picked her up, I could see lice crawling around in her hair. I didn't know how to help. One time, I stayed late with a kid who told me that his parents hit him, and I had to call Children's Aid Services. I tried not to freak out when the neighborhood kids pulled together an epic skate jam, with skateboarders flying through the air out of a tiny bowl next to the fountain. I felt completely out of my element when I showed up to work one morning to find a sizable drunk man passed out in front of the door to the center. Parents came and dropped their kids off, so I led circle games outside until the police arrived and heaved the man into the back of a truck, then drove him off to the drunk tank. The kids ran inside to play, completely undeterred by the insanity of what had just happened.

Downtown Hamilton woke me up from my small, insulated suburban world, revealing that while my privilege had kept me physically safe, it had also left me disconnected. For the first time in my life, I felt like I had found a geographical place that mattered to me, and I realized that summer that I had a role to play in its healing and flourishing. It took years before I really understood the city and its neighborhoods. It took even longer for me to truly become a part of it. But something had sparked in my sixteen-year-old heart. I knew that this was my city and I was supposed to love it and serve it.

But at the time, I was clueless as to *how.*

When I was twenty years old, I finally made peace with becoming a pastor, and shortly after, I learned about "church planting," which is when a few people start a new congregation with a mission to love and serve a particular place. That's when everything began to click. I had run from pastoral ministry because I didn't want to sit in a church building all day and listen to middle-class people tell me about their problems. But being deeply immersed in a neighborhood, witnessing what God was up to, and seeing a new congregation emerge from the soil—that was exciting to me.

How was it that I had spent twenty years in the church and never considered the relationship between faith and geography?

Once our eyes are opened, it's impossible to miss it.

Place Matters

One of the most overlooked themes in the whole Bible is "place." Israel's story begins with God calling a man named Abram to leave his father's land and go to a particular place. For his descendants, the land is about much more than real estate; it's linked to the very promises of God. Generations later, when the Israelites are conquered by other nations and forced to leave their homes, they weep and lament. They aren't just leaving their property; they're also leaving their tradition and story. The land is tied to their identity.

The emphasis on "place" carries through to the early church. When I was a kid, I always assumed that the names of biblical books like Ephesians were some sort of code, probably in Latin, for something mysterious and spiritual. Years later, I learned it was just a letter written to a church in a city called Ephesus. Even Jesus, who traveled and proclaimed the Good News, limited his geographical scope to a few places. He didn't march into Rome, where he could have influenced the powerful, or journey into foreign lands, where he would have had a cool accent. He traveled to Jewish cities, to his own people and culture, and called them to join what God was up to.

Place matters.

The church used to know this. For most of her history, she was more than just a house of worship; she was the hub of an entire community. Church buildings were the place where neighbors connected, where art was created and shared, and where all people, regardless of their class, could find a home. But as cars became the default mode of transit, and suburban development sprawled farther and farther, we saw the birth of a new sort of church. Suddenly, people joined a congregation based on preference, driving to whoever had the best pipe organ or the most accurate theology. Sure, it might be a little farther away, but what's a half-hour drive when you're used to a forty-five-minute commute?

Most of us live, work, play, and pray in different directions, traveling vast distances every day, and this can lead to a disintegrated life. We probably travel farther in a month than our great-grandparents did in their whole lives. Our culture has become disconnected from the land in which we live—with food, clothing, and technology shipped in from around the world. This is before we even consider the internet and how, for the first time in human history, hours of our day are spent in the void. We receive an endless stream of tweets, articles, videos, and podcasts without knowing the culture and context they came from. Don't get me wrong, I love the internet and don't know how I'd do the dishes without podcasts. But there is a lot of evidence to suggest this rootlessness isn't good for us. It can leave us disjointed and displaced, longing for a connection to the geography we physically inhabit.

How can the church help us reconnect to place?

When I went to seminary, I developed a singular mission: to learn all I could about starting a new congregation in downtown Hamilton. At the time, my wife, Meg, and I were newlyweds living on the campus of a private Christian college in the countryside. It was the opposite of Beasley Park. If we were going to plant a church that reflected downtown Hamilton, it would need to look radically different from the farming fields around us or the suburban church culture I had grown up in. It needed to be distinctly urban.

Undeniably Very Cool

To learn more, I took my first internship at a decade-old church plant called FreeChurch Toronto, which everyone called FT for short. Now, as a general rule, when people tell you they are part of a "cool church," you should laugh in their face. There is no such thing as a cool church, and if you claim to be one, it is the first sign that you are most definitely not cool.

But FT was *actually* supercool.

When we first visited the church, it was unlike anything I'd ever seen. They met in a magnificent cathedral in the middle of downtown Toronto on Sunday evenings. They used custom-built spotlights and hung light bulbs throughout the cavernous space to illuminate the room and cast shadows. One time, they made the whole sanctuary sparkle as if we were underwater, and they projected four submerged faces on the walls of the sanctuary because . . . art? I still don't really get it, but it was undeniably very cool.

Each week, the senior pastor, David McGhee, preached sermons that were part poetry, part *This American Life*, and part old-school

Baptist revival. To this day, I'm convinced he could have read from a phone book and made us all cry. But more than that, David *embodied downtown Toronto*. From his off-kilter sense of humor to his fixed-gear bicycle, he effortlessly translated the ancient traditions of the Christian faith into a modern expression. At no point was this more clear than when he broke bread for Communion. Every Sunday, when he went up to introduce the Eucharist, David would hold the bread high over the congregation, his voice cutting through the darkness:

"On the night he was betrayed, Christ took bread, and after giving thanks, he broke it, saying, 'This is my body, broken for you.'"

And then he ripped it clean down the center. Holy bread dust fluttered through the air, descending onto the congregation, raining down like manna from heaven.

I got chills.

A few weeks into my internship, David sidled up next to me in my pew: "Makins . . . this week, you're breaking the bread." I walked in front of the congregation, hands shaking, armpits sweating, heart racing. I looked out into this crowd of very cool, very intimidating Torontonians and, with a false confidence, lifted the bread high and proclaimed with a cracking voice: "*This-is-the-body-of-Christ-which-is-broken-for-you . . .*"

But when I went to break the bread, I realized that something was off. I had watched David effortlessly introduce Communion but now realized I had never paid attention to his *form*. The thing about talking into a microphone with one hand while holding bread in the other is that you likely only have two hands. Now, any regular person would have taken the obvious next step, which would have been to put the microphone down on the table and break the bread, of course.

This is what I should have done. This is not what I did.

Instead, I proceeded to (I can't even believe I am writing this out for the whole world to read right now) put the bread under my sweaty right armpit and use my free hand to rip the loaf clean in half.

"The body of Christ, *broken for you*!"

In the moment, I didn't even realize what I had done. I had blacked out in the Spirit. It wasn't until I sat back down that Meg pointed out to me what had happened, and I wanted to melt through my pew. When I cleaned up at the end of the service, I took note of the Communion table. Half of the bread was gone, consumed by the congregation, while the other squashed and damp piece of Christ's body had been pushed off to the side completely untouched.

Three weeks at the cool church and I had already proven I was anything but.

Bottom Up

One month into my internship, David announced he was stepping down from pastoring the church. I was devastated. I wanted to learn how to embody a city, preach like a poet, and break bread without ruining everyone's appetite. Stepping into his role was Cyril, a very tall, redheaded rapper who taught Koine Greek at my seminary and was writing his PhD thesis about "The Confluence of Poetry and Philosophy in St. Anselm's Theology." You can't make this stuff up.

The goodbye party for David was one of the first times we got to connect with people from FT in a non-Sunday setting. Lingering near the wine table, we met Joel and Anne, who had just finished recording their first country album together. We met Andrew and Esther: she worked for a local nonprofit, and when he wasn't leading worship at the church, he had a day job making music out of random objects for people on the internet. We met Dylan, the graphic designer–mystic; the Broadbent sisters, who made dazzling pieces of art using only blue ballpoint pens; and Brad, a CG animator who once spent a month working on just the left eye of the hunchback from the movie *300*.

The way they lived in their city was unlike anything I had seen before. None of them owned cars; instead, they biked for transit.

On the weekends, they hung out in public parks and ate at locally owned restaurants and coffee shops. Initially, I tried to figure out how FT had created this unique community, but it wasn't long before I noticed that the culture of the church wasn't shaped from the top down but from the bottom up. People biked everywhere because Toronto parking was too expensive, they hung out in parks because their apartments were too small to host parties, and the cafés were locally owned because big chains didn't want small storefronts. It was the limitations of downtown Toronto that had created something so unique. It wasn't that FT was trying to be cool and artsy; FT was just a church that reflected its cool and artsy city. The church had created a context for these local people to come together, and once they did, an eccentric community began to grow out of the soil.

"You and Meg should move to Toronto so you can become the associate pastor of FT," Cyril said to me over coffee as my internship placement came to a close. "The church loves you and it would be such a great opportunity." I drove home from the meeting with my head spinning. I had taken this internship to learn how to pastor so that we could start a church in Hamilton. But why not work full-time at an already established church in Toronto? I love my city, but people find us on a map by looking "near Toronto."

Shouldn't we go where we can have the largest impact?

Re-Placing

Every church is limited by geography. Some try to kick against these constraints by streaming their Sunday service online 24/7 or launching a new campus every six months. But at FT, I learned that it's in embracing our limitations, not ignoring them, that we most organically see goodness grow.

Once we accept the "place" our church inhabits, we can begin to notice all the natural ways our geography overlaps. When we realize someone in our church lives in the same apartment building we live in, that our kids go to the same school, or that we bike the same route to work, cultivating community becomes much more natural. We begin to connect in the spaces that make sense for our shared context, whether they are public parks, coffee shops, or strip malls.

As we do so, we can further integrate our church with her geography.

Here's a simple example for anyone who is part of a congregation. Every church I know has a Sunday coffee time. What beans do you use and where do you buy them? Most of the time the answer is "the cheapest beans from the closest supermarket." But what if you ran something simple like coffee through the lens of place? What is the closest local shop that roasts coffee beans? Could your church build a relationship with that shop and become a consistent buyer? How would that help you connect in your neighborhood? Could you learn more about the beans, where they are harvested, and the people involved in the process? Maybe even send a letter to the farmers in Nicaragua to thank the producer for all their work? How would they feel knowing their work helps you all fellowship, and how much more appreciative would you be for every cup from that church carafe?

If you find yourself cheering at that idea, why don't you run with it? My guess is your pastor is flustered, and your setup leaders are busy. So just ask someone in leadership if you could make it happen. In nearly every case, I bet you'll get a positive response. It might cost a little more money, but you could put out a donation jar to help cover the difference. It will take time and mental energy, but what a beautiful way to take something simple and turn it into an integrated celebration of church and place.

Of course, our churches could run all sorts of things through this grid. What would happen if we organized small groups based on neighborhood? If we cut out a few of the "Top Worship Hits" and sang more locally written songs? What if there was a team of people who prayerfully baked fresh bread on Communion Sunday? These small shifts can create a church community that feels homegrown.

Doing things locally will always require more intentionality and will often be more costly, but no one person is responsible for all of it. We each have a small part to play.

This is also true when it comes to pursuing justice in a broken world. The internet has allowed us to see the suffering of everyone, everywhere, all the time. But in most cases, we can do little beyond donating some money or signing a petition. The irony is that there are a handful of local issues in our own backyards that we could have a huge impact on.

When we integrate church and place, things get practical very quickly. We talk about helping refugees in Syria, but church says to us, "There's a family from Liberia just down the street." We post online about global conflict, but church says, "There's a neighborhood association that needs a new member." We want to educate the world, but church reminds us, "There's an after-school tutoring program on Tuesdays."

So where is your place? It's probably closer than you think. We can be quick to romanticize other locations and downplay where we are, assuming if we could just *get somewhere else*, we'd find our calling. But more often than not, our place is right under our feet.

In the late 1980s, a nun named Sister Mary traveled to India to meet with Mother Teresa, who spent her life ministering to the poor in Calcutta. Sister Mary had thought she would join the famous nun in her mission to the poorest of the poor. But Mother Teresa's advice surprised her. She said, "No, I want you to go back to your neighborhood, find the poor, find your own Calcutta."

So when Cyril generously offered me the job in Toronto, I had to graciously decline. We weren't Toronto. We were Hamilton. We had already found our Calcutta.

Descending the Mountain

A few months later, we were driving down Barton Street, the poorest neighborhood in Hamilton, looking at houses with my parents.

One of the benefits of moving into a historically impoverished area is that you can buy a home right out of college. The challenge is that you have no idea what is dangerous in a "this is fun and different" way and what is dangerous in a "you will probably get stabbed" way. My parents drove us from open house to open house, wearing pained expressions of concern, a hesitantly supportive "Are you sure you want to make this horrible mistake?" look on their faces.

After seeing one house we liked, we drove down the neighboring street, past a bunch of abandoned businesses. Meg was trying to be so optimistic. "Well, look at *these* little storefronts!" she said, pointing at the boarded-up shops. "I bet someone could start a neat business in there." Spotting a group of ladies, she celebrated the organic community life on the street, neighbors just walking around and chatting with friends. My mom turned to look at the group, and as she did, one woman straight-up *punched* the other one in the face. She spiraled through the air and landed hard on the ground. Immediately, her friends jumped the aggressor, forming a pile, and a street fight broke out on the sidewalk in the middle of the afternoon.

We didn't put an offer in on that house.

We eventually settled on an old brick home just a few blocks east of Beasley Park, where I had first fallen in love with downtown. Our backyard butted up to a furniture factory loading dock. Next door, our Jamaican neighbors blasted reggae, played dominoes, and smoked a lot of weed. On moving day, my little cousin observed that our neighborhood looked like a city she'd visited on her mission trip to Honduras because "there are kids running around without shoes on and lots of stray cats!"

Her observation wasn't inaccurate. Downtown Hamilton had scared me when I was sixteen. But I had spent enough time in it to see below the surface, to notice its beauty and resilience, and to be pulled into it. Now we had our own little piece of the city to steward, a home where we would host dance parties and sing-alongs and from which we would launch a new business and a bike-lane campaign. The house in which, just a few years later, a small circle of friends would gather, praying and scheming about starting a new church.

It was time to put down roots and see what would grow.

3 THE "RIGHT" WAY TO START A CHURCH

Even the Son of God needs a break sometimes. After a day filled with miracles, including the soon-to-be-famous "feeding of the five thousand," Jesus sends the disciples across the lake by boat. Then he heads up a mountain to pray. As the disciples are sailing, the wind becomes choppy and the waves beat at the side of the boat. Before long, the only audible sound is the rain drumming the deck, broken by the occasional crack of thunder. Some disciples slip and fall, struggling to find their footing, while others try to regain control of the ship. Now, these disciples are good Jewish boys who were raised hearing stories of chaotic waters and sea monsters, and they are not interested in becoming Leviathan's lunch. They work all night, fighting against the tempest. By morning they're exhausted and the storm has yet to break. Clothes soaked through, muscles aching, they strain their eyes to see land. Instead, they see a shape on the water. What is that? Another boat . . . or something more sinister? A demon? A monster? A ghost?

They settle on ghost and enter full hysterics. It's bad enough to be shipwrecked, but now they're also being haunted. But as the spectre moves closer, they begin to get some clarity. It's not a ghost at all; it's a person. It's . . . *Jesus*? Yes, Jesus is casually walking on freaking water, in the middle of a storm. "It's just me. Don't be afraid," he says, while literally doing the strangest thing a person has ever done. And if you're a disciple, you've got to be so relieved by this turn of events. "Hooray! Jesus is here!" They remember how, just a few months before, Jesus had calmed the water with his words. This time he's walking on the water, so it's safe to assume he's got this covered. The disciples are embracing one another, laughing, and recovering their breath. Except for Peter. Peter is still staring, fixated on the shape of Jesus. He yells out something so strange, so stupid, that it made history: "Lord, if it's you, call me to go out on the water with you." And for a moment, no one moves, no one speaks, the storm beats against the silent boat. Jesus responds with one word: "Come."

Peter walks to the edge of the boat, the sea spitting up to meet his face. He puts one leg onto the ledge and, without a moment's hesitation, leaps into the darkness. But there is no splash, no cold water consuming him. Instead, he finds resistance, like jumping onto a firm mattress. The waves lick his ankles and his feet shift to find balance, but after a moment, he stands confidently and begins his steady walk toward Jesus.

It's safe to assume Peter had never walked on water before. He hadn't been trained for it. All he knew was how to take the step that was in front of him and then the one after that. Each stride must have been terrifying but he kept going, and before long, he was experiencing a miracle.

In Over Our Heads

Twenty friends squished into the tiny living room of our one-hundred-year-old, creaky house. We were meeting for the first time to pray about starting a church. Meg and I were still trying to figure out how all this had happened so quickly. She and I had met the first day of college, were dating by second year, and, by some combination of true love and Christian guilt over making out all the time, were married by fourth year. During the first year of our marriage, I put over sixty thousand miles on our secondhand Honda Civic driving an unholy triangle between seminary, my internship at FT in Toronto, and night shifts at a group home. But once we made the decision to move downtown, the path forward was set. We spent all our free time getting to know the city.

Meg had opened a children's clothing store on one of downtown's "up-and-coming" streets (which is code for "totally boarded-up" streets). Through it, we got to know a lot of young parents who desperately wanted to connect with other people. One of them, Sandra, had experienced a pretty rough year. She and her husband had recently separated, leaving her with two young kids and a lot of hurt. Meg would listen well and try her best to be like Jesus.

Hanging around and trying to be like Jesus sort of became our thing. We'd go to neighborhood meetings and street parties, political rallies and trendy bars, and whenever someone asked what I did for work, I'd smile and say, "We're starting a church!" Most of them stared back, confused, and replied, "Why would anyone do that?" But *on rare occasions*, someone would say, "I used to go to Mass as a kid" or "I've been meaning to sort out some spiritual stuff." Even Sandra, who was raised in a secular home and educated at a liberal university, started asking, "When is this thing going to start?"

Which brings me back to the circle in our living room. Around it were a few religious dropouts who were hesitant to reengage, some friends who had moved to our city after being priced out of Toronto, and a few spiritual nomads, uncertain about committing to anything. All of us had issues with church, but it just seemed too easy to walk away. We knew that we needed community, to be connected to something ancient and rooted, and despite all the church's imperfections, it's not like we had some better idea. In theory, church seemed great: a community of people following Jesus together, forgiving sins and breaking bread, loving God and blessing neighbors. Who wouldn't want to be a part of that?

But I had spent enough time in the city to notice that the existing church was failing to connect with lots of people. There were creatives who believed the church was too rigid in her expression, young people who saw it as trying to re-create the past, and misfits of all stripes who believed the church didn't want them for a variety of reasons.

It wasn't like my nonreligious neighbors had no interest in churchy things. Most of them were *spiritual people* who wanted to be part of a *community*. But it seemed like church, which ought to be the perfect place for *spiritual community*, just wasn't a fit for them.

Perhaps they sensed something Christians have often missed.

Over the past few decades, many faith leaders have observed that no church is neutral in terms of its culture. The language we speak, the style of music, even the room we meet in communicates a certain way of doing things. In most North American Protestant churches, the cultural assumptions are predominantly white, traditional, and middle class. This isn't inherently evil, but Christians have often assumed it is inherently good. All of the existing Hamilton churches were reaching people, but when my friends walked into those spaces, they felt like they were "culturally commuting" to be there, visiting a place on Sunday that didn't share any overlap with the other six days of their week.

We didn't know what the culture of this new congregation would look like, but I had to believe that if we were patient, it would eventually grow up from our common soil, just like FT had in Toronto.

But we had no idea how to get this thing going.

What we currently had was a group too small, too young, and too stupid to know what we were doing. At twenty-three years old, I was the senior of the group and still couldn't sync my online calendars. I looked around for anyone who could help us track a budget or take minutes during a meeting. All I saw were artists and millennial hippies.

"Can anyone help us make a budget?"

"I can *dance* you a budget!"

We were in over our heads. Although, in my experience, that's when God tends to show up.

The Storm

Have you ever tried to walk on a slackline or a balance beam? The instinct is to stare at your feet, shifting your weight in an attempt to find stability, but it's almost impossible to keep your balance if you look down. The only way to keep standing is to focus your eyes on an object ahead of you, like a tree branch, a bleacher, or the face of a beloved friend calling you out into the storm.

The clouds overhead are dark, illuminated only by momentary flashes. But Peter doesn't notice, his eyes still fixed forward, one foot moving in front of the other. Then a strong breeze hits him from the right, his soaked cloak whips to the side, and suddenly he realizes that what he is doing is crazy. He looks around and begins to panic, fears racing through his mind: *I'm walking on the water! The storm is getting worse! I'm too far from the boat!* And like ice straining under too much weight, the surface of the water cracks and breaks, plunging Peter into the cold. He tries to swim, but his clothing is wet and heavy; his muscles still ache from a night of fighting the storm. His mind fills in the details of the deep dark below, swarming with sea monsters. The disciples are watching from the boat, shouting as loudly as they can through the storm. Peter can't hear them, as the water drowns out the sound. His lips chatter, his vision fades, and he slips below the surface. And then in a moment—BAM! A hand reaches down, grips his forearm, and pulls him up and out of the depths and back onto the waters. Now standing on the sea, the storm still raging around him, Peter looks right into the eyes of Jesus. With rain running down his dark skin and through his beard, Jesus says with a gentle smile to Peter, "Little-faith one, why did you doubt?"

Following Jesus is supposed to be an adventure. It involves taking a risk and stepping into the storm. But in North America, the church hasn't been known for this. We've had large buildings, political power, and packed services, and we've gotten comfortable. We've shifted toward preservation, assuming the church will always have packed sanctuaries and full-time staffing. It's not that any of this is particularly bad—I'm a pastor and my family appreciates having health insurance—but the *assumption* of comfort frightens me.

You know what the early followers of Jesus assumed? That they'd be crucified. That's a very different career path.

But as the North American church faces decline for the first time, all of this is changing. The way we've always done things is no longer working, the empire of Christianity is eroding before us, and we'll need to radically reimagine what it means to be the church in the modern world.

And I thank God for this, because the church has adventure in her DNA.

Jesus lived his life wandering from city to city, telling stories and confronting injustice and evil. After his resurrection, the disciples were on the run, founding communities of resistance all across the Roman Empire. Disciples of Jesus have kept faith in the most oppressive and violent conditions imaginable, from a German seminary resisting the Nazi party to illegal underground churches in China. The church journeyed around the world and carried in her the unchanging Good News of Jesus and his resurrection. But the culture of Christian community has always been changing. It's dynamic and responsive. And now it's evolving yet again.

We weren't made for safety and security.

We aren't meant to preserve the status quo.

Jesus wants us to walk right into the storm.

The Right Way to Church Plant

The group that had gathered in our living room was excited. After just one prayer night and a picnic in the park, we were convinced we should start meeting on a Sunday. We optimistically set a start date just one month away. With the countdown on, I began trying to connect with some other churches in the area. We wanted to start a different sort of church community and had no interest in "sheep stealing" or competing. If we were lucky, some other congregations might even befriend us. I had heard about a local network called TrueCity. It was composed of fifteen Hamilton churches from different denominations who had, for over five years, set aside their differences in order to join God in his mission. When I found out that many of the pastors gathered monthly, I asked if I could meet with them and share a bit about our experimental church plant.

The meeting was in a coffee shop downtown. When I arrived, the couches had been rearranged into a circle and the group was in lively conversation. They were talking about a study that had just been released, which revealed that the average life expectancy in some downtown neighborhoods was the same as in many developing countries. The group was spitballing ideas on how to confront these challenges. While they talked loudly and gestured with their hands, one person scribbled in a small notebook, clearly trying to make something out of the pastors' ramblings. Occasionally, he would attempt to tie the group's ideas together into something coherent, his speech peppered with quick "yo's"—a holdover expression from ten years of missionary work in the Philippines. This was Dave Witt, who had initially gathered a few churches together to engage in justice work. Years later, it had grown into the TrueCity movement, which he was reluctant to lead. But his humility backfired. Everyone loved Dave so much that he was jokingly given the nickname the Bishop of TrueCity.

"This is Kevin and he is planning on planting a church so, yo, I wanted him to share the story here," said Bishop Dave, introducing me to the group. I filled them in on the story so far and mentioned we were going to start Sunday gatherings in a few weeks.

One of the oldest and wisest pastors in the group spoke up. "Kevin, you have so much passion, but that's not the way you start a church," he said, shaking his head. "Gather a core team, but don't launch publicly right away. It will *kill you* to pull Sundays off, and you won't even know what your church is really about! Take a year—a full year—and just meet in your living room. Talk about your vision and clarify what God's calling you to do. Write down your core values, mission statement, and vision documents. Apply for some grants, get financial pledges from the congregation, and rent a good building. Set up your children's programs, organize a band, launch a website with parking details . . . and *then* have your grand Launch Sunday! That's the right way to church plant."

Risky

There is a risk that comes with stepping into the storm. What if you aren't able to walk on water and your friends have to help you? Or you make it partway before sinking, and you're unable to get back to the boat? But there's another risk that we don't often talk about, one that most people in our culture are completely blind to: the risk that you'll live your entire life on the boat, so busy making plans and strategizing that you never actually try walking on water.

Perhaps you know how that feels. You have ideas about what you'd love to do to love God and your neighbors, but all of it is terrifying. So you push the desire away and decide that you'll just read a few more books, watch a few more YouTube tutorials, and get a little more mentally prepared before you take the next step. But sometimes God is calling us into an adventure that we can't prepare for.

Ask any parent when they felt ready to raise a child and you'll get the same answer: they never were. You just have to figure it out as you go.

Head knowledge has its place, but we learn best by diving in.

This looks different for each one of us. For the disciples, it looked like feeding five thousand people by day, wrestling a storm by night, and walking on water by morning. For you, it might look like mentoring someone in your church, cleaning up garbage in your neighborhood, or volunteering at a local organization. Making art, starting a business, or fostering children might be your storm.

Whatever it is, there are three things I know for sure:

1. You'll never be fully prepared, so get ready to jump in.
2. You don't have to do this alone; the church is on mission together.
3. Even if you start to sink, Jesus has you.

He's promised that if we step into the storm, he will be with us, and even if we begin to sink, he will grab on to us. This isn't our mission—it's Jesus's storm to conquer—but he invites us into the adventure so that we might have a life worth living.

He wants us to experience the thrill of walking on water.

So when the wise pastor told us it was too soon to start Sunday gatherings, I knew immediately that he was correct. Better to keep things small for a year or so. That felt manageable, safer, and . . . comfortable. Too comfortable. It didn't feel like walking on water. I wasn't scared of us drowning—Jesus caught Peter when he was sinking. What scared me about his advice was that we'd spend so much time charting a course from within the boat that we'd never actually jump over the edge.

We completely ignored the pastor's advice and started meeting three weeks later.

Hipster Factory

On a Sunday afternoon in September 2010, Eucharist Church gathered for the first time. The word *Eucharist* comes from the Greek *eucharisteo*, meaning "to give thanks," as Jesus did when he lifted up the bread and wine during his last supper with the disciples. We wanted a name that would invoke this meal imagery, a bunch of oddballs gathered together around a table with room for everyone. The fact that the name was old and religious-sounding also proved a nice juxtaposition to the space in which we met. We had rented a reclaimed factory space, now home to a few artists and a boudoir photography studio. It had hardwood plank floors, crisp white walls, and an old cage elevator. It was a hipster church dream. The official reason for bucking the conventional morning-church time slot was to connect with a different type of spiritual seeker, but off the record, it was equally about being able to sleep in on Sundays.

The circle of friends from our living room was at the space, setting up chairs and making coffee in our "welcome lobby"—a hallway that housed exactly one sofa. Our service was going to start at 3:30 p.m., but we'd open the doors half an hour earlier to have a preservice coffee time for what would hopefully be at least five visitors. I was busy puttering around the "sanctuary." A fashion studio the rest of the week, the room was now filled with donated rickety chairs, and extension cords snaked in every direction. One cable ran to our brand-new projector, balanced Jenga-like on a stack of books atop an already wobbly table. Troubleshooting the sanctuary caused me to entirely lose track of time, so when I walked into the welcome lobby at 3:10 p.m., I expected to see our core group working away. Instead, I found pandemonium.

People sat on the floor, drinking coffee, while others sprawled on the lone couch. Out front, one of our team members waved in visitors from every direction. Children were jumping off the stairs, shaking the old building on impact. One kid was outside, inviting a woman in a Playboy Bunny costume to church (I wasn't joking about the boudoir studio). A woman from our core team was frantically washing mugs *in the closet* because that's where the only sink was. Everyone was hugging, laughing, and trying to breathe. Don't get the wrong idea; we weren't some sort of overnight megachurch. This isn't *that kind* of church story. We just rented a really small building.

All the same, a good sixty or so people had shown up, and I ran around trying to get a sense of where they had all come from. Some were family and friends supporting us in our first week, others we had met through city connections, and one group had been part of a church plant that had recently shut down. They'd heard about us through the TrueCity network. As everyone funneled into the fashion studio and squeezed onto the secondhand chairs, I even noticed Sandra from Meg's clothing store. She had snuck into the back row, one kid balanced on each knee. We sang loudly that first Sunday, feet stomping along to the music on the old hardwood floors, the building itself physically shifting under the pressure. The projector crapped out at one point, and it was way too hot in the room, but it didn't matter. We had taken the next step. Now it was time to see who else wanted to jump in with us.

After the service, we invited those who were interested to stick around for dinner and learn more about what we hoped Eucharist Church would become. Now there were thirty of us, once again sitting on the floor in a circle, having upgraded from an old, creaky house to an old, creaky factory. It was finally time for me to pitch a compelling vision of what Eucharist Church would become.

"We know our city needs a new church with a culture that feels homegrown," I said, full of conviction, "but we don't know what that looks like yet. We're sort of taking this one step at a time. But if you get the sense that God is nudging you to join us, we'd love to have you." There was a short pause before the reality check: "We have no setup leaders, no small groups, no kids' volunteers, and no money. No one else is going to be the church for us. If we want to be the church, *we* have to own it together." I ended with as vulnerable an ask as I could muster: "So I guess . . . if you're in . . . we need you all to sign up for a role right now, start giving financially so we can meet our rent, and commit to showing up every Sunday as well as in one another's lives during the week."

I looked around the room, expecting to see horrified faces completely overwhelmed by the task ahead. Instead, they were leaning in, eyes wide open, heads nodding in approval. The call to adventure had woken up some deep desire in us.

We wanted to walk on water, and this was our storm.

4 FAITH IS COMMUNAL

The room was full of holy energy. When we sang, people stomped their feet so loud the whole factory shook under us. Every Sunday, more visitors showed up and we did our best to make space. One week, a young woman almost fainted, which our charismatics saw as a sign of the Holy Spirit's tangible presence. Turned out she just needed air. One of our worship leaders, who had been involved in a church plant before, pulled me aside to offer an insight. "This won't last," he said to me, pointing at the overstuffed factory room. "Right now we're experiencing a high, but it won't stay like this forever." And then he gave me the weirdest, most helpful mental image:

"Kevin, right now a cat could fart into a microphone and people would fall down and call it worship."

He was right. The "Sunday show" was going great, but eventually this energy would fade, and what would we be left with then? I knew church had to be more than a weekly gathering but wasn't sure what we were supposed to do next.

At first, I was convinced we had to find ways to be a good Christian witness to the city. So we ran a steampunk-themed summer camp, which featured an "Imagination Train" maintained by a bunch of twentysomethings in thrift-shop overalls. We hosted the Blessing of the Bikes, in which dozens of riders received a springtime prayer for safety before riding en masse through the city streets, following a pedal-powered stage that housed a brass band. One Sunday, we took photos of every congregant with their hands covered in fake blood in front of a large golden halo. Then, hoping to spark conversations about faith, we pasted eighty of the photos onto an old fence at our city's Art Crawl event under the title *Sinners and Saints*.

And while all these events were fun, they weren't exactly working in the way I had hoped they would. We didn't have new neighborhood people showing up on Sundays, and those inside our church were growing fatigued by my never-ending onslaught of one-offs. Even I was growing tired of constantly pointing to the next outreach ministry on the horizon. Inevitably, each event would come and go in a flash, and then it would be in our rearview mirror, an object growing smaller and smaller with each passing Sunday. We'd be left more tired than when we began, without any lasting impact to show for our efforts.

Those involved in justice work were having a similar experience. People in our church had jumped into important causes like affordable housing and mental health support. They joined food co-ops and bike co-ops and housing co-ops and pretty much anything that referred to itself as a co-op. We campaigned against a downtown casino and pioneered a cycling campaign, which resulted in the longest urban bike lane in the province.

And while all of these initiatives were beautiful, we quickly realized they weren't the answer. People would burn bright for their cause and then promptly burn out. We knew how to petition against a casino, but we didn't know what to do after we had won the fight.

Church had to be about more than just hosting events or pursuing justice.

I was talking with Bishop Dave about my frustrations, when he told me about how he and his wife had recently visited the Philippines—fifteen years after they'd returned to North America. They had been missionaries there for a decade and were excited to revisit the organizations they had started and the people they knew. "It was so encouraging and *so* frustrating," he told me. "No one remembered anything we had worked on! We had built teams and started new ministry projects, and no one talked to us about *any of that*. All they remembered was that we played LEGOs with them, had a *Where's Waldo?* book, and pumped water from the same well they used every morning."

He leaned forward: "No one remembered what we did. They only remembered who we were."

Skinny Jeans

When we first moved downtown, Meg wanted to find new ways to put down roots and make friends. She'd heard about a craft night that happened at a local bar downtown. She showed up one night, by herself, and ended up getting woven into the coolest craft collective ever. They spent their evenings knitting, sewing, and cross-stitching a Hamilton revolution. On Christmas Eve, Meg got a phone call. Glancing at her phone, she saw it was from Jamie, another member of the craft collective. She picked up the phone and said hello, but Jamie had already hung up. Meg tried calling back, but no one answered. A few minutes later, the phone rang again, and Meg heard crying on the other end of the line. "Hey . . ." the voice sniffled out through tears. "I'm sorry to bother you on Christmas Eve, but you're the only person I know who prays, and I was wondering if you could pray for me." She told Meg that her marriage was in a really hard spot and she needed someone to pray for her. Because they had spent hours at a bar, knitting together and hanging out, Jamie knew Meg would be that person.

A week after the phone call, Meg and I were invited to a big dance party at a friend's studio, and we were so excited to skip it. The exhaustion of Christmas travel had worn us down, and we were desperate for a cozy night in. The popcorn was popped, the movie was ready to go, and the sweatpants were on—and we all know that once the sweatpants go on, they don't come back off! The phone rang. It was Jamie. "Are you guys coming tonight?" she yelled, barely overpowering the bass beat in the background. "Sorry, Jamie," replied Meg, who was, in that moment, the queen of comfort. "We decided to just take it easy tonight." There was a brief hesitation before Jamie responded, "Oh, that's okay. I was just really hoping to see you guys tonight and talk more about all this stuff going on . . ."

Meg and I took one look at each other, and we knew what we had to do.

We stopped the movie, took *off* our sweatpants, squeezed into our tightest hipster jeans . . . and partied for Jesus. We danced for hours and talked all night, working through the kind of big questions that only surface when you're exhausted from dancing and covered in sweat. Sitting on the curb at 4 a.m., we broke bread—greasy pizza, in this case—together. Jamie and her husband were pulled into our lives and, through us, into a wider church community. Her husband started coming on Sundays and met other men who had gone through similar challenges as he had. Through them, he learned how to own the mistakes he had made. Jamie and her husband were not only able to forgive one another but they also were able to reconcile their marriage.

They never did "join" Eucharist, but we brought church to them. Beer and pizza were our bread and wine. Street curbs were our altar.

It wasn't about what we did but who we were.

Four Friends

When the word gets out that Jesus is back in town, the entire region comes to see him. Before long, the house he's in is so packed that no one can even get on the property. People are poking their heads through windows and climbing on shoulders just to hear one of his stories. Those outside the home notice a small group in the distance, carrying something between them and moving quickly despite the heat. "You should have come earlier if you wanted a seat," someone shouts to them as they get closer. "Unless you're carrying a pile of gold on that mat, you ain't gettin' in!" But the truth is that they had started scrambling as soon as they'd heard Jesus was back in town—the four friends working to track one another down before heading to the fifth, who is always at the same place: the city gate.

The men are carrying their friend, who has been unable to walk for as long as they have known him. To be paralyzed in any culture is to face unique challenges, but in the ancient world, without social assistance or accessibility laws, it was difficult to even survive. Unless you had people who cared for you. Being resourceful fellows, they decide to bypass the front door entirely, instead boosting one another onto the roof of the clay house and carefully hoisting their friend up as well. Inside, the people try to ignore the sound of footsteps on the roof, but when dirt begins to fall onto their heads, it proves impossible. Looking up, they see cracks forming as chunks of clay begin to fall, and before they can even piece together what's happening, a human hand has burst through. The ceiling is quickly being replaced by daylight, which is then interrupted by a large shadow. Something is being carefully lowered down.

If I were Jesus, I would have been *livid*. Many scholars believe that Jesus is hosting this teaching in his house. My old house is already leaking as it is. If a few strangers ripped the roof off because they didn't want to wait for me to come outside, I'd be threatening to sue. But Jesus isn't mad. While others run for cover, he smiles wide and shakes the clay dust out of his hair. When the man finally lands before him, the whole room is silent.

Jesus looks up to the four friends whose heads are now peeking in from the corners of his new sunroof and, having witnessed their faith, he heals the paralyzed man.

But wait, that can't be right.

The author must have meant that when Jesus saw *the paralyzed man's* faith, he healed him. But that's not what the text says. It says that Jesus saw *their* faith. Plural. The faith of the paralyzed man's *friends* made *him* well. The Gospel accounts are filled with stories of people helping one another experience Jesus's healing. A Roman centurion has enough faith to heal—not himself but his servant. A woman has faith to heal her daughter. Faith is never an individual exercise. There's a reason Jesus didn't select one good student but instead called twelve apostles and seventy-two disciples. It's the same reason the early Christians clustered together and formed the church. It's why the Nicene Creed doesn't begin with "I believe" but "We believe." Why the Lord's Prayer begins with "Our Father who is in heaven," not "My Father who is in heaven."

Faith is a communal endeavor.

Communal Faith

Those of us raised in North America have inherited what might be the most individualistic culture in human history. We were taught to be successful, to climb the ladder, to go after the best schools, internships, and job opportunities. But this hyperindividualism has backfired on us.

You may not notice it right away. If you're still in school or just entering the workplace, you likely have a flood of new relationships in your life. But in your twenties, and especially in your thirties, you might start noticing how difficult it is to sustain community. You may have spent evenings at the bar with friends, but that changes when some people marry and have children. The coworkers you used to get lunch with eventually move on to new opportunities, and getting together becomes nearly impossible. I once read a tweet that said being friends as an adult is just saying, "'We should really hang out more' over and over again until one of you dies." This isn't to say it's impossible to form community in the modern world. It's just *very* difficult. Many of the institutions that used to cultivate relationships, like clubs and churches, are on the decline, and a lot of people feel most known in online spaces, where relationships are mediated by a screen. Even governments are responding to the lack of community in our cities, with the UK electing a minister of loneliness—which was my nickname in middle school.

It can be hard for those of us raised in this individualistic culture, in religious traditions that esteem a personal relationship with God, to catch these references to a faith that is fundamentally communal. But it's a vital part of why church is so important. In the New Testament, the word translated as *church* is the Greek word *ekklesia*, which means "called-out ones." When we hear the word *church*, most of us picture a building or a worship service, but she isn't a location or an event.

The church is a community called out of the normal way of living in order to follow Jesus. Church isn't something we go to at all, she's something we are a part of.

Once we rediscover this side of church, so much begins to fall into place. Many of us were taught that we needed to believe the right things to belong in the church, but maybe we don't need to have all our intellectual opinions sorted out before we start to follow Jesus. If church is a community of people called by God to move toward Jesus, then it's perfectly acceptable to walk with others in that direction, even if you don't know what you personally believe. Eucharist Church celebrates Communion every Sunday afternoon, and we are quick to remind people that this table does not belong to our church. It's Jesus's table, and he welcomes all who desire to come to him, whether they have a lot of faith or just a tiny mustard seed of belief. What's important is that we come to Jesus's table together and bring him what we have. Feelings and intellectual opinions will come and go; they aren't a good foundation for a life of discipleship. But when we bind ourselves to a group of people who have committed to move toward Jesus together, we no longer have to be anxious about what we feel or think in any given moment. We can trust that those around us will help us get to Christ, and as we grow and mature, we'll even be able to help others.

Four friends carried their friend to Jesus, and two thousand years later, our small church start-up was learning to live out a communal faith.

Weird

The church has so often been busy chasing the next trend, but in this splintered and fractured culture, maybe we need to back up and reclaim the one thing we've always been decent at: getting people together so that community can grow.

This might happen by doing a check-in with each other in mid-week small groups. Or at a morning parents' hangout: one hour of adult conversation when life mostly consists of changing diapers. We may meet up for noon prayer times or special services. One of the best ways to grow in community is to join God in his mission by helping refugees settle, tending a garden, or volunteering in a prison ministry.

At the very least, we should gather once a week. Every Sunday, followers of Jesus get together in real time and in a physical place, so that we can eat, learn, pray, and sing. In our digital age, this might be the most radical and subversive thing we do. The internet allows us to listen to the best sermons in the world, stream our favorite worship music, and hang out with like-minded Christians on Twitter. While all of that is valuable, it's no replacement for a room full of real people trying to follow Jesus together. When we gather, we may sing songs we don't like or include people we wouldn't choose to hang out with, but that's what makes it so powerful. It's not about how great the "Sunday show" is. If the liturgy fumbles or the sermon is boring, we know that it's only a small part of the bigger mission of forming a community of Jesus followers. Besides, you can always download a better sermon when you get home. What a time to be alive!

The Sunday gathering isn't everything, but it can create a context where people can connect, out of which friendship and community can grow.

Maybe we've just forgotten how radical the small things are.

A few years after Eucharist launched, we had a woman join us for the first time. She had never been to church before in her life. Afterward, she told me she couldn't believe what she had experienced: "I came with my young son into a beautiful old building, then someone offered us fresh coffee and some snacks. We met a few new people and sang some beautiful songs before a volunteer took my son into the back hall to do crafts so I could listen to a lecture about the most interesting person who ever lived. Afterward, someone brought my kid back to me, happier than before; we got a little snack of bread and juice; and then, as we were leaving, someone asked if we wanted to eat dinner with them and some friends in the park. Oh, and all of that was *free*? Are you kidding me? *Nobody does stuff like this!*"

She gave me fresh eyes to see the beautiful thing that was right in front of me.

I could go on all day about the issues in the church. Joining one is probably going to put you in community with some really annoying and judgmental people, but that's not uniquely a church problem. There are jerks everywhere. Sometimes I'm one of them. But for all her faults, we can't forget the beautiful things about church. Even in her simplest elements. Praying for one another, carrying each other's burdens, finding an apartment for a family in need, or bringing a casserole to a new mother: these are pretty countercultural. I went to a rock-climbing gym for two years, and no one invited me to a small group. It's not *normal* to welcome strangers to your table, into your home, or into your heart. But that's our calling as the church.

We carry one another to Jesus.

Sandra

Sandra showed up the first week Eucharist gathered. She's the woman my wife had met at the kids' clothing store who had recently separated from her husband. Her only experience of church had been the occasional visit with her grandparents, so she had expected to be one of the youngest in the room. Instead, she found herself the resident senior at thirty-two. She thought about making a run for the door, but there was no way to elegantly sneak out of that packed room with two children in tow. She was stuck with us. I remember looking out during the sermon and seeing Sandra sitting with a kid on each knee, surrounded by peppy college students and disheveled artists, with tears running down her face.

Sandra came up for Communion that week and spent the next few months trying to understand what it meant. She was logical and liberal, educated and progressive. She was very comfortably not religious. And yet, she couldn't deny that *something* was interrupting her life in a real way. She continued to show up every Sunday to a room full of strangers who were becoming something more. She connected with others in the church and shared some of her story. She was being carried to Jesus by our little community of faith—a friend on each side—which allowed her to experience the sort of healing and forgiveness only he can give. And as she became aware of the grace she was receiving, she was able to extend it to her estranged husband.

We baptized Sandra a few months later. Standing in a small dunk tank, she shared her story about how God had inconveniently and wonderfully knocked her off her feet and into a new life. Then I asked her a series of questions, concluding with, "Who, Sandra, is your Lord and Savior?"

She laughed out loud with tears in her eyes. "I can't believe I'm saying this . . . Jesus Christ is my Lord and Savior!"

"Then, Sandra," I replied as I fought back tears myself, "based on this confession, we baptize you in the name of the Father, the

66

Son, and the Holy Spirit!" Sandra fell back into the water, and for a moment all was still. Then the silence was broken by the sounds of her reemergence. Everyone lost their ever-loving minds! There was cheering and clapping as her husband walked forward to embrace her. And there, in front of their church, they renewed their wedding vows . . . while she was still dripping wet from her baptism.

You can't make this stuff up.

Afterward the entire church came forward to pray for her family. We laid hands on Sandra and her husband and on the kids, too, who stood in a small puddle at their mother's feet, trying to figure out what exactly was going on. There was a collective "Amen!" and a holy moment of silence, broken by the voice of their five-year-old son, who shouted at the top of his lungs, *"But what about the bread?"*

I could have paid him! Great question. What *about* the bread? I hopped up onto a pew and held the bread high in the air, and the whole community came together around the table.

Now, I've been a pastor for ten years, and let me be clear: you don't get Sundays like this all the time. But sometimes you do. And when you do, you have to tell others about them, and you have to give thanks for them. This was one of those mountaintop moments I will never forget.

But church isn't a moment in time. Church isn't a story in a book. She's a living community.

Which means she will continue to grow and shift and change and be utterly unpredictable. As you read more of our story, you'll see that I'm speaking from experience on this one. Community is messy. There will be flashes of glory and seasons of grief. Some will find faith and others will lose it. People will heal one another and harm one another. Nothing stays the same.

So you have to remember. I remember the smell of the sanctuary. I remember the wet carpet beneath our feet. I remember the five-year-old voice calling us to the table.

And I give thanks. Because without moments like this to look back on, I'm not sure we would have made it.

5 THE NIGHT THE CHILDREN NEVER CAME

"And besides, when else is everyone in the neighborhood just outside meeting one another?"

Thus ended my pitch for the first Eucharist Halloween park party.

Some Christians have conflicting feelings about Halloween. It probably has something to do with the fact that children literally walk around dressed up as the devil. This hesitance has led churches to do all sorts of weird, alternative Halloween events. These range from totally not Halloween "harvest parties" to outright soul-disturbing "haunted hell house" evangelistic outreach events in which children are led, Dantesque, through a low-budget representation of hell, complete with the youth pastor screaming in a vat of red Jell-O and an altar call at the end.

Don't believe me? Google it and prepare to hate everything.

Of course, much of this drama is for naught. Halloween is typically far more innocent. It's kids hoarding thousands of tiny chocolate bars, waddling door to door in costumes that were stitched together by exhausted parents at 3:00 a.m., while excited strangers say, "Wow! What are *you*?" to a kid who is clearly Iron Man.

This was a chance for our little aspiring church to get to know the people of the neighborhood. The factory we had been meeting in was directly across the street from the city's largest park and was just begging for a party.

We bought a ton of candy, set up some games, and created a small All Saints' Day candle display. And it was awesome. Dozens of families visited, playing games, eating snacks, and lighting candles for the dead. We got to connect with all sorts of people we never would have met otherwise, and they had their first positive impression of our church.

But here's the thing. In the church world, if you do something once and it's a success, you now have an annual event on your hands.

Cue the subcommittee.

One year later, we had moved out of the claustrophobic factory space and into an old church building on the other side of the park, which provided far more space in which we could prepare this year's Halloween party. We spent weeks in the church basement crafting cardboard robots that would fill the park. We bought even more candy, prepped twice as many games, and, by popular request, tripled the amount of All Saints' Day candles. We huddled together in the park and waited for the waves of children who would come and enjoy the fruit of our labor.

And . . . no one showed up.

I'm not even kidding. No one. Not even the kids from our own church! It was like every child in the city was in cahoots to make us miserable failures. In the end, it was just a bunch of grown-ups in face paint, standing next to cardboard robots, holding candy in the dark.

We called this ill-fated evening: "The Night the Children Never Came."

At this point, one year in, everything we had touched had turned to gold. We had thrown parties, baptized people, and hosted events, and everything had been a huge success. This was our first flop. The following Sunday, those who hadn't been able to make it waited with bated breath to hear how our latest community event had gone, and we had to tell them about how badly our party sucked.

We started telling ourselves this story every time one of our ambitious projects tanked. We'd look at each other and shrug our shoulders: "The Night the Children Never Came."

Unfortunately for us, years later we can confidently say this is not the only time we've flopped. Here's a horrible reality: sometimes you study as hard as you can, you write the best grant proposal, you organize the teams, you raise all the money, you promote the event with every resource . . . and you still fail.

Sometimes you give it your all, and it just isn't enough.

You Feed Them

Being a disciple of Jesus must have been frustrating at times. You'd think that it was mostly one-on-one mentoring meetings and small-group learning exercises. Instead, the crowds just kept finding him and taking up his time. On some pages of Scripture, you can almost feel the disciples' frustration. A few chapters ago, I alluded to this now-famous story in Jesus's life, but in case you need a catch-up, here are the footnotes: Five thousand men come to see Jesus with their families in tow, begging for teaching and healing, and hours later the disciples are fed up and frustrated. One of them, who is particularly organized and responsible, has run through his checklist, crunched the numbers, and realized that they have no food to offer a group this large. He begins to stumble through the crowd looking for the other eleven before finally approaching Jesus with his little notebook in hand. "Um, Rabbi, I think it's time we send this crowd away," he says, looking around at the unfamiliar faces. "It's getting dark, and they should probably go find someplace to eat." Without missing a beat or dropping his voice, Jesus turns to the twelve and replies, "You feed them." The disciples turn to one another, confused, before one speaks up. "Lord, it would take more than half a year's wages to feed this whole group; we can't possibly get enough food to pull this off."

And then Jesus asks an uncomfortable question:

"Well, what do you have?"

They huddle together and pull what they've got out of their pockets before turning back to Jesus: "We've got five loaves . . ." one replies, and then another chirps, "Oh! And we have two fish!" with great optimism. And you've just got to picture Jesus staring at the disciples, twelve grown men holding up a few tiny loaves and a couple of dried-up fish, knowing it's hardly enough to feed *them*, never mind the thousands in the crowd. But he witnesses them bringing what they have, simple as it may be, and a smile breaks out on his face.

"I can work with that."

You probably know how "The Feeding of the Five Thousand" ends. It's sort of in the name. The crowd breaks into small clusters, the disciples pass out the food, and in some mysterious way, there is more than enough food for everyone to eat. I've heard conservative Christians argue that we need to be able to defend the logic of these stories, but it's hard to do that because they defy explanation at every level. Some liberal scholars suggest that, in seeing the disciples offer up what little they had, the crowd was also struck with generosity and began to empty their pockets, which is a lovely sentiment but entirely stapled onto the text. However you understand these stories, they can offer new insights into what it means to live in the world as God sees it. When it comes to the feeding, I am always struck by Jesus's words to the disciples, so blunt and bold: "You feed them." To which I would have responded just like the disciples did: "Are you freaking kidding me? I don't have the money, ability, or capacity to pull this off!"

Whenever you or I hit our limit, Jesus asks us the same question he asked the disciples: "What do you have?"

Sometimes it's not much. When friends struggle with their mental health, we sit with them, not knowing what to say but having ears to listen. Someone in our community is deep in grief, and while we can't fix it, we can take our beat-up car and go get their groceries for them. A couple in our church recently moved into a new apartment and needed help getting it ready, so a few friends showed up to help. One of them spent hours painting the bathroom. He was completely out of his element. It took him forever to cover one wall, and there were streaks everywhere. But in that moment, he gave what he had in order to bless his friends. And the friends graciously received his gift, even if someone else had to do the final coat.

We bring our loaves and fish forward, hand them to Jesus, and trust that he can use them.

But trusting *Jesus* with our resources means releasing *our* expectations. We show up to where God has called us and give all the energy we've got, but the results are completely out of our hands.

Surrender the Outcome

I'm a pastor, so part of my vocation is to preach sermons. Sometimes I have sermons that I've slaved over all week, and at the end, I say to myself, "This is a killer sermon." I won't shut up about it all weekend, and I drive Meg crazy as I buzz around with energy and just sort of yell the sermon's concept at her. Then I strut into church on Sunday and spit that hot sermon fire from the pulpit. And it's like a beautiful gospel dove that I release into the congregation. *"Be free, beautiful dove!"* I cheer, throwing the bird into the air. It arcs high above the congregation, the light shimmering through the majestic white feathers . . . before it falls to the ground and lands with a THUD.

The sermon flops. Just dies instantly.

I've preached great sermons that nobody cared about. People have come up to me in the Communion line immediately afterward and tried to talk about binge-watching some new TV show.

And then there have been times when I have dragged a limp, dead sermon with me into the pulpit. To say I "preached" it is to do a disservice to the art of speaking words. The first time this happened, I felt like I had just spent thirty minutes drooling a sermon out of my open mouth and all over the congregation: "Ya, there was a guy . . . Jesus . . . and he was, like, God? And God . . . loves you? And has a . . . plan . . ."

All the energy of a constipated slug.

And afterward, there was a line of people waiting to talk to me. "Oh my word," a young woman said with tearful eyes. "That sermon was so moving." And I was like, "No, it wasn't! That was an oratorical catastrophe!" Then she responded, "When you said, 'Jesus shows us what God looks like with skin on,' it just changed everything for me." And internally, I'm screaming, "I've said that a million times before! That's the incarnation of Christ! What made this time so special?"

I've preached substandard sermons that produced beautiful new insights.

I've preached great sermons that turned to vapor in the air.

Because we don't get to control what our work does.

We have to entrust it to someone else.

It's kind of pathetic and embarrassing, isn't it? But isn't it also really good? Because, I don't know about *your* story, but I'm not always winning.

In the culture around us, it's outcome that is praised. Your salary, your final grade, your job title, what house you live in, and your superficial beauty. Nobody cares about whether you gave it your all or if you improved over time. By high school, they've stopped handing out participation awards. But in God's reality, everything is flipped upside down. God isn't impressed with our achievements;

he's looking for people who will show up and bring what they've got, even if they don't have much.

My expectation for our second Halloween party was that we'd offer God our prayer candles and big, dumb cardboard robots, and he'd give us a bunch of new families and some media coverage. Instead, what God gave us was an exercise in how to name our failure and laugh about it. And while I would have loved a success story, I can't overstate how helpful "The Night the Children Never Came" has been in shaping the culture of our church. It gave us permission to celebrate simply showing up and bringing what little we have. And perhaps that's what we actually needed.

Participation

When I think about the disciples offering up their scraps, I wonder why Jesus bothered to involve them at all. He was the human representative of the one true God. The same God who rained bread down from heaven for the Israelites and sent ravens to deliver food to the prophets. Surely Jesus could have called on his Father to take care of business without involving a bunch of slow-witted disciples?

My friend told me about how his two-year-old daughter now helps prepare breakfast for the family. He puts a peeled banana on the cutting board and then steps back so she can chop it up. "She is terrible at it," he said to me beaming with pride, "but I just think 'Wow! Look at you *trying*!'" I think that's how our heavenly Father sees us. He knows that we like to help cut up the banana, and he knows that we suck at it. We slow the whole breakfast prep down. But he'd rather make the meal *with us* than simply bring it to us on a platter. He wants us to be a part of the healing of the world, and so he stands off to the side and cheers us on: "Look at you trying!"

A few years ago, I was preaching on this idea of bringing what we have. To make sure the point hit home, I ordered a hundred participation ribbons—the kind I used to get after an entire season of mediocre basketball—and handed them out to everyone in the congregation. One by one, people came forward. I looked them in the eye and said, "I hereby award you this participation ribbon for bringing what you have to our church."

I gave one award to a man on the poverty line who struggles with serious health issues and takes a long bus ride across town to join us every Sunday. I gave another to a woman who carefully budgets every penny to ensure she can give what little she has to God's work in the world. Still another was awarded to a single parent who moves heaven and earth to get a babysitter so that he can attend small group every other week.

The church doesn't put winners on a podium. She has no interest in who comes first. She's the one place in town still handing out participation awards.

The other week, I was at the house of someone in our congregation, looking at their children's art on the fridge, when I noticed the white participation ribbon held up by a magnet. It must have been up there for years, a constant reminder that we bring what we have and then wait to see what God will do.

Salad Dressing Blessing

When we first started Eucharist, the church was cool and hip. And then people got pregnant. Nothing ruins your hipster credibility like baby puke stains and mandatory background checks for Sunday school volunteers. It started with one couple and then a second and a third. In year two, we had four women who were pregnant at the same time. The next year, we had five at once. We called these early pregnancy booms "Baby-pocalypse"—but eventually we realized it wasn't going to slow down. We were living in the end times. While they took away some of our cool factor, our young ones gave us so much more. They brought new noise, new life, and an endless stream of baby dedications. For those of you not in the know, a baby dedication is the adorable ritual of corporately loving a squishy little ball of new life. We bring the family forward to dedicate the baby to God, and then we as a church dedicate ourselves to that family. We end by putting olive oil on the baby's head, a sign throughout Scripture of God's blessing, and we march the baby around the sanctuary. It's a pastoral highlight for sure.

One Sunday, we were set to dedicate two babies, one of whom was the newborn of a refugee family. I wanted the family to really feel loved as we formally welcomed their child into our church and into our country, so I worked hard all week to ensure the sermon and dedication weaved together perfectly. But the morning of the double dedication, something was off . . . inside of me. My stomach was doing spin cycles and my whole body was secreting sweat. I tried to give myself positive reinforcement as I drove to the building: "I am going to church, I am going to preach this sermon, and I am going to dedicate these babies." An hour before the service, I hobbled into the building like the Hunchback of Notre Dame, carrying a little bit of olive oil in a mason jar for the baby dedication. I was limping through the front hall, toward the sanctuary, when that week's setup leader, Sue, interrupted me. Sue is one of those people who will call it like they see it.

"Kevin, what are you doing here?" she said sternly. I raised my head up high and stoically responded, "I'm just feeling a little out of it; I'll be fine." She looked me up and down. "You're gray," she observed clinically. Then she sent me home.

And that is how, for the very first time, I called in sick on a Sunday.

Thankfully, our church is full of insanely gifted and generous people. With a few phone calls, we had the whole service covered. Stephen, a wicked smart seminary graduate who writes code for a day job and pours so much energy into our community, said he'd preach a sermon he had been kicking around, and Bishop Dave was willing to lead the baby dedication. Responsibility-free, I drove home, head spinning and forehead sweating. I stumbled through the doorframe and hobbled to the couch, where I fell backward into the abyss.

Cut to black.

I woke up five hours later. My eyes were all gooey, and my mouth felt like it had been rubbed with moldy sandpaper. I called Stephen to ask how everything had gone.

"Oh man. Everything was great, although there was one thing that was a little interesting."

Stephen told me that, during the last verse of the song before the baby dedication, he and Dave realized they couldn't find the olive oil we use to bless the babies. They should have known I'd left the jar of oil in a nondescript plastic bag under the pew in the back corner of the dark hall. Obviously. With the dedication about to begin and no oil to be found for the blessing, Bishop Dave panicked. "Don't worry," Stephen said with a confidence he had no right to possess. "I'm on it."

Stephen ripped out of the hall and into the kitchen, scanning for olive oil. He looked on the countertops and the table near the front door. There was no sign of it anywhere. But in the kitchen was a gigantic fridge, which held random items left behind after church potlucks. His eyes caught a bottle on the second shelf:

"Greek & Feta Dressing."

It just so happened that this dressing had been sitting in the fridge long enough that the contents had separated from one another; the spices settled on the bottom and the oil on top . . .

"That'll do."

With surgical precision, Stephen poured out the top half of the dressing, ran back into the room, and passed the bowl to Bishop Dave, who was already midway through the dedication. He raised the bowl, dipped his thumb into it, and rubbed premium spiced oil all over the foreheads of the babies. Making the scented sign of the cross, he recited words of blessing: "May the Lord bless you and keep you. May the Lord make his face to shine upon you and be gracious to you. May the Lord look upon you with his favor and grant you his peace."

A salad dressing blessing.

Now this is a classic Eucharist story. It's got all the components: running behind on time, split-second problem solving, innovative liturgy.

Does it reveal our disorganization? Yes.

Does it make me laugh every time I think about it? Yes.

But here's the real question: Were those babies blessed and welcomed into the family of God? You better believe it.

Jesus asked us, "What do you have?" And our answer was "fear and anxiety, good intentions and some honest prayers, one failed Halloween party and half a bottle of salad dressing."

Then a smile broke out on his face.

"I can work with that."

6 NAP SUNDAY

We were a few years into our church plant experiment before we realized Eucharist's schedule was too full. There was always another social event or upcoming meeting, never mind the never-ending onslaught of Sundays, each of which were supposed to be more spiritually impressive than the last. It wasn't just the congregation's schedule that was overstuffed. As a young, energetic pastor, I was putting in forty or fifty hours of mostly unpaid work every week. I funded this lifestyle by working full-time night shifts at the group home, all while finishing off seminary so that people wouldn't know that I was actually a small child, entirely in over my head. I was hustling for the Lord and actually felt *proud* of how busy I was. My body, however, refused to play along, and my eye began to twitch randomly. For a while, I assumed this was normal, until I talked to a few friends in health care who assured me that eyes never spastically twitch because things are going well.

The writer of the book of Hebrews compares our life on earth to running with endurance the race that is marked before us. I was a marathon runner sprinting through my youth, and if something didn't change soon, I was going to seriously hurt myself.

But it wasn't just me. Every person in our community was feeling overstretched, wondering if laundry and taxes and budgeting and church life and getting kids fed and unclear work expectations and commuting and seeing family and side hustles and sports leagues and maintaining friendships were even possible to fit on the same calendar.

And all of us, when asked how we were doing, responded with the same words:

"Good, I'm just so . . ."

Busy.

Our culture has an addiction: we crave a full schedule. In this way, Eucharist was no different from the world around us. We got hooked on being busy, and we had barely even noticed.

The church I was raised in had a totally different pace.

She followed the "church calendar," an annual rhythm observed by congregations around the world, which moved through seasons such as Advent (the month leading up to Christmas) and observed special events like Pentecost Sunday (remembering the coming of the Holy Spirit). Nothing was urgent to the Lutherans. Instead, the Christian life was scheduled, decades in advance, into a sacred Day-Timer. Dates were set aside for baptisms and Communion, with preaching texts prescribed by a rotating three-year lectionary. When I first became an intentional follower of Jesus, I looked back on the "church calendar" with judgment. It appeared rote and lifeless, too rigid to be relevant in a world that needed the gospel. I was convinced Christians needed to move faster, be more efficient, and make more happen.

But I was an idiot.

Special Days

In a world of increasingly full calendars, everyone wants their slice of the schedule.

Music labels create social media campaigns and drip-feed singles to the public in order to keep ears on their artists. We used to watch our favorite sports teams compete for just a few months of the year, but now fans need to watch the pre- and postseason recap, pay attention to draft picks and speculation, and engage with podcasts and web forums throughout the week. New blockbusters fight to be associated with their season, billed as the "must-see movie of the summer" or the "perfect Christmas film." Viewers are so relieved that, though work may be stressful and the ice caps are melting, at the end of the month we get to see the superhero punch Evil in the face.

But it doesn't end there. Have you noticed how many "days" there are now? We've got the classic staples (Mother's Day, Labor Day, Thanksgiving), but then we've got all these new holidays trying to stake their territory like National Pi Day, Make a Difference Day, and Bike to Work Day. Every time I log in to social media, some group is telling me how today is a *very important day* for their cause and that I should educate myself, share their links, and probably donate money to prove I'm not part of the problem. Have you ever seen one of these "days" and wanted to yell, "*That's not a thing!*"? A few weeks ago, I was informed it was National Grilled Cheese Day, which, of course, was being promoted by a multinational corporation that sells single cheese slices.

I'm not suggesting that Christians can't eat grilled cheese or go watch the newest blockbuster movie, but we need to be aware of the war over who gets to control the precious 365 days on the calendar.

Because it is a battle.

Every spring, a large coffee chain hosts an event in which participants have a one-in-infinity chance of winning a television and a slightly better chance of winning a coffee that tastes like hot cigarette water. It was only in the last few years that I realized the campaign coincides perfectly with Lent. Because how could anyone give up coffee for forty days when they could win a two-dollar donut? Even more sneaky is the way religious holidays are subtly transformed over a long period of time into something entirely different. Easter, which celebrates that Jesus rose from the dead, is now about a human-sized bunny rabbit who lays chocolate eggs. Advent, the season leading up to Christmas, has become a month in which everyone talks about presents. Christians have historically thrown hissy fits over whether companies put "Happy Holidays" or "Merry Christmas" on their disposable cups—failing to notice that businesses only use our sacred language if it proves economically beneficial. Corporations don't worship the baby in a manger, even if they put out decorations.

Look just below the surface and you'll see that every religious holiday has been co-opted by the culture around us to become about profit and profile, consumption and comfort.

That is, all of them but one.

You Are Going to Die

Perhaps it's good news that we can never fully escape our family of origin.

It wasn't until Eucharist hosted our first Ash Wednesday service that I recognized how much the Lutheran church of my childhood was tied into our church plant's spiritual genetics. Ash Wednesday is a serious contender for the weirdest thing churches do. Seven weeks before Easter, Christians gather to have ashes placed on their foreheads in the sign of the cross and to hear someone say over them, "Remember, you are dust, and to dust you shall return." Which is spiritual talk for "You are going to die."

"Then what happens?" you wonder. And the answer is: nothing. That's the end of the service. You don't even wipe the ashes off your forehead. You just carry on with your day, buying avocados at the grocery store with a cross on your forehead like a sixteenth-century monk.

And that's what makes Ash Wednesday the only religious holiday no corporation wants. You can't sell "Remember, You're Going to Die" cards.

The good news of Ash Wednesday comes after the bad news. It invites us to remember our frailty, count our days, and then put our trust in Jesus, who has overcome death. After our first Ash Wednesday service, a few people in our church talked to me about how refreshing it was to celebrate a sacred day free from the hype and noise of our culture. It became our gateway drug into the rest of the church calendar.

Our Catholic friends must have thought we were adorable, poorly observing Lent and butchering Epiphany. "Look at these spiritual mutts, *rediscovering* the church calendar!" But there really was an internal shift occurring within us. Everyone still listened to podcasts and binged television series, but it was no longer the way we marked our time. These sacred seasons had given us a different rhythm.

Lest we get too idealistic, it's worth noting that the church has historically controlled time in a manner not unlike modern corporations. I suspect that seven hundred years ago, people anticipated midnight Mass much like we anticipate a new Marvel movie. So yes, even if the intent of the church calendar was to point people to the life of Jesus and into community, the church still became influential and wealthy as a result. But few congregations today wield that sort of power, and good riddance. The church is at her best when she's countercultural and subversive. We don't need to plan a political campaign in order to destroy National Bagel Day and bring Lent back to the masses. Let the politicians and corporations fight on social media over the special "days" of the year.

We pledge allegiance to a different schedule.

One year, we preached through the assigned Scripture readings of the church calendar. That first Sunday, our pastoral intern, Leshia, got up to preach. She talked about how our faith has often helped us reclaim *places* by using candles and incense and hosting meals, but the church calendar took it one step further.

"The church calendar is how God reclaims *time*."

Ordinary Time

God's mission to reclaim time calls us to occasionally pick up some practices (generosity, prayer times, church services), but I was surprised by how much it tells us *not* to do.

For example, one of the commandments in the Hebrew Scriptures is to take a sabbath day of rest. One day a week, God's people are to do nothing productive. Instead, we are called to rest in his goodness and provision.

Christians typically sabbath on Sunday, but since that was a workday for me, Meg and I needed to find another day of rest. Friday was our best option, but it would be difficult to pull off. Meg had sold her business when we started Eucharist and was working full-time in an office. To request a four-day workweek could backfire. Even if they said yes, we were looking at a 20 percent pay cut. For two kids in their early twenties, still trying to get a church off the ground with a bunch of college debt, this was a sacrifice. But something had to go on the altar: either our mental health, marriage, and souls . . . or a slice of our paycheck. Once we saw it that way, it was an easy decision. I can't overemphasize how much sabbath has saved us. One day a week, we walk instead of drive and go to the local coffee shop to play cards with friends. In the words of Eugene Peterson, we "play and pray." On Fridays, I refuse to talk about Eucharist, and the congregation quickly learned how to honor my decision. I used to get texts on Friday afternoons asking me church questions. Those would be immediately followed up by another text: "I'M SO SORRY, I FORGOT IT WAS FRIDAY—DO NOT READ THAT TEXT!"

Admitting our limitations gave others in our community the freedom to name their own, and over time, the sabbath worked its way into the culture of Eucharist, even impacting our congregational schedule.

The longest season in the church calendar is called "ordinary time." It runs for roughly half the year. For a few months, nothing particularly special happens. The church simply counts the weeks and catches her breath. We decided to practice ordinary time over the summer months by allowing our Sunday services to get really chill. We had no kids' program, no projector, and no speakers set up. We met outside in the garden and ate watermelon in the sun. We kept the service to sixty minutes and capped the sermon at ten. Essentially, we went full Anglican. We also set up a preaching guild of speakers who would step into the pulpit for eight weeks, which gave me the freedom to just be a part of the community. After two weeks, my eye twitch went away.

We live in a culture that is constantly trying to entertain us, competing for our attention and offering us an endless stream of new products, each better than the last. That is why it was so important that ordinary time be thoroughly unimpressive. I am of the firm opinion that, every now and then, church should suck. The music should be out of key, the sermon meandering, and the chairs uncomfortable. That is our reminder that church isn't a Sunday show—just another product to consume—but a called-out community of people following Jesus together. That's easy to forget if church is "good" every week.

Sometimes things just need to be ordinary.

Keep Time Together

What's your relationship with time? Is your calendar always demanding more of you, or is it helping you enter into God's "unforced rhythms of grace"? Something we've learned is that you can't reclaim time alone; you need to do it in community. This is yet another area in which church can be very helpful. We can encourage one another to take a weekly day of rest, we can anticipate together during Advent, and we can fast together during Lent.

The church was meant to keep time together, but we've often resisted this gift.

Some congregations view the church calendar with suspicion, afraid to put ashes on foreheads because it's not strictly biblical. Perhaps that's the attitude of the congregation you are currently a part of, and you find it frustrating. The good news is that every church already lives out of an alternative schedule. Rather than switching congregations or trying to force an entire church to change, what if you start by noticing all the ways you are *already* taking part in God's redemption of time?

For example, every church I know gathers weekly for a service. In doing so, they set a new rhythm for life, one that marks time not by hockey practices or Friday night happy hour but by the gathering of the saints. This alone should preach to us: the culture that gave us "TGIF" believes the weekend is our reward for a job well done. We have to earn our rest. What is fascinating is that, in the Christian tradition, we gather to worship on Sunday, which is the first day of the week. We begin our week with rest because God's grace is given before we do a thing to earn it. The Good News we receive on the first day ought to empower us for the following six.

I'd put money on the fact that the church you're a part of already observes Easter and Christmas, so lean into those times. Celebrate them as milestones in the year. Gather your friends or your small group together for foot washing on Maundy Thursday, even if it's not a formal church event. During Advent, attend another congregation's midweek service together. You don't need permission to eat pancakes in your living room or go on an Epiphany hike with your neighbors. You can follow the church calendar exactly where you are.

Of course, there is rigidity on both sides of the coin. I've spoken with plenty of "high-church" people who wish their congregation would stop being so stuffy about the church calendar. Some traditions feature an obscene number of holy days, each of them requiring attendance, and before long, everyone is just exhausted.

This is why it's important to remember the church calendar wasn't designed to be a new law. I'm reminded of Jesus's words when he was questioned about his lax attitude regarding the sabbath: "The sabbath was made for humankind, and not humankind for the sabbath."

We need the freedom to play with the church calendar, to bend it, innovate within it, and let it live in fresh new ways today.

After all, *it* was made for *us*.

Nap Sunday

The Sunday after Christmas is a pastor's hangover. Most of them selflessly allow the intern to preach to a crowd of thirty-two exhausted parishioners who really just wanted to stay home but felt guilty because they heard their dad's voice in their head, saying, "If God can show up in a manger all the way from heaven for you, then the least you can do is drag your butt to church."

A few years into Eucharist, as the post-Christmas season got closer, I panicked. We had gone all out during Advent, literally building a grand apocalyptic Christmas monster and decorating the old sanctuary in neon gaffer's tape. Having barely survived the insanity of the past month, the idea of diving into some new sermon series just a few days later completely overwhelmed me. I looked to the church calendar for help and found . . . nothing. Not even one "just take it easy" week. I thought about just canceling the service so we could all catch our breath.

But it got me thinking: if the church calendar was made for *us*, could we add our own holy days? The community had spent weeks driving around to visit family and friends, and everyone was still bloated from turkey and stuffing. Christmas had exhausted us.

I decided we would have a Sunday service but promised it would be different.

When the congregation arrived, we sang a few quiet songs and prayed together, but when it was time for the sermon, everyone found their own pew in the old sanctuary. They lay down and settled in. Then the lights turned off and everyone napped for thirty minutes. This, my friends, is how we invented Nap Sunday: the height of holiness, the peak of the liturgical year, and a sacred day we totally made up.

Throughout the nap, we had a few people go up to the microphone and read Jesus's words from the end of the Sermon on the Mount: "Therefore I tell you, do not worry about your life, what you will eat or what you will drink . . ." Finally, after thirty minutes of sleep, we turned on the lights and people began to rise from their slumber. They rubbed their eyes, stretched out their arms, and came forward to receive Communion, having learned nothing new. Because that's the whole point of the gospel: We don't need to accumulate information. We don't need to self-improve. We don't need to earn a thing. All is grace.

So take a nap.

Nothing

In the years since we started it, Nap Sunday has become a phenomenon. People bring pillows and invite their friends. They wear onesie pajamas. I even made a poster that reads: "KEEP CHRIST IN NAP SUNDAY!"

Some congregants who were unmarried when Eucharist started now have babies lying on their chests, rising and falling with every breath. Others in our community have health issues and can't lie down easily, so they sit in the darkness, taking in the stillness and silence. Kids lie restlessly on the ground, rolling back and forth until they settle into the deep, uncommunicable peace of God. Someone in the shadows begins to snore loudly, which is perfect. Nothing says grace like snoring in church.

I take a moment to look around the room during nap time, trying to be attentive to what God is quietly doing.

A woman sits in the back row, left side, staring at the stained glass images on the wall. She thinks about her mother, who died about eight months ago. The last remaining parent, the last physical link to her own family heritage. She thinks about the previous eight months and how much work it was to clean her parents' property before listing it for sale. She reflects on her organizing of old files and articles, even coming across her father's old Bibles. She thinks of her own journey away from and back into faith over the past twenty years. She remembers that her mother and father attended a church just like the one our community rents, how they sat in a pew just like this pew. She takes note of their absence. The loss of love, of physical touch and phone calls, concerns and check-ins. She hasn't had time to sit with her grief. She's been too busy to stop.

Life doesn't slow down when a parent dies. It speeds up. She still had to go in to work and walk the dog and cook dinner, all with the added burden of making arrangements for a funeral and dealing with the house and reconnecting with distant family and stewarding dozens and dozens of brown cardboard boxes containing what once was a life.

She thinks of all this, sitting in the dark, surrounded by the sound of saints breathing quietly and steadily all around her.

She thinks of the presence in this space. The presence of children and young adults, some who have lost their parents and others who are her parents' age. She senses the presence of the One who holds it all together.

She tells me later that she cried through the entire nap. She tells me she hasn't had time or space to slow down or be still until now. She tells me how grateful she was for a time where there was nothing.

I assume everyone wants a great sermon. She reminds me that what people really need is time.

Four people read the peaceful words of Jesus, and she weeps between each reading.

The lights slowly rise, and all around her, people begin to sit up. She sneaks out to the washroom, cleans off her streaks of mascara, and finally comes forward to receive Communion without having done a single thing to earn it:

"The body of Christ, given for you."

7 THE KINGDOM OF GOD IS LIKE A POTLUCK

The first Sunday of every month is potluck week at Eucharist Church. As Eucharites stream into the building, carrying slow cookers and tinfoil-wrapped goodies, many of us try to guess what's going to be on the menu in an hour. We also have a shortened service on these weeks because no one wants to listen to me ramble on when the smell of brisket is causing them to salivate. One week, I decided to try something different. Rather than prepare a full-length sermon, we'd do a group activity to try to answer a question people had been asking for years: What are the religious backgrounds of people in this room?

The first voice yelled out, "Latter-day Saints." Then Anglican, Anglo-Catholic, atheist, and Reformed—which begged the question: "What kind of Reformed?" A few people scattered throughout the congregation helped to clarify: Christian Reformed, Canadian Reformed, Dutch Reformed, and Reformed Church in America. All of which are obviously completely separate from one another.

Now the floodgates had opened: Pentecostal, Baptist, Orthodox Presbyterian, Associated Gospel Church, nondenominational, agnostic Jewish, a-different-kind-of-Baptist, Mennonite, Lutheran Church in Canada, Lutheran Church—Missouri Synod, Roman Catholic, Missionary Alliance, Jesus People 1970s movement, Brethren, United Church of Christ, yet-another-kind-of-Baptist, and, of course, someone was raised in "a secular but spiritually rooted hippie commune."

This is who we are at Eucharist.

Our congregation is a mixed bag of spirited misfits, each of whom has their own messy story to tell. Now, *in theory*, gathering all these spiritual nomads is beautiful and healing, but the reality is a whole lot messier. Most of us are used to viewing the world through a tribal lens, choosing to spend time with people who have similar backgrounds to ours or who believe exactly what we believe.

But increasingly, these old tribal lines are fading.

I am more and more convinced that my generation doesn't really care which denomination has the most accurate theology or the most beautiful buildings. There may be a few places where people are loyal to a denomination from cradle to grave, but that's not what I'm seeing. In my experience, people who were raised in the church are sick of the fighting, and those who weren't raised in the church don't even know what we're fighting about. There was a time when there were so many Christians that every time we disagreed about something, we could just split the congregation in half. But in a world of radical church decline, that's no longer a viable option. In secular environments like Canada, Europe, and most large American cities, there just aren't enough Christians to start making other Christians our enemies.

And this is resulting in a monumental family reunion.

Every few weeks, I get another email from a community of Jesus followers who are mixing together traditions and expressions. All around the world, streams of Christianity are converging and invigorating one another.

But all this diversity does raise a practical question:
How do we stick together when we're all so different?

Katy's Question

Eucharist was knee-deep in a sermon series on the book of Jonah when I sat down for coffee with Katy, a highly educated young woman who had been visiting our gatherings for a few weeks. It was the first time she had ever been in church. "Okay, I've been taking notes," she said, opening up her journal, "and I have a bunch of questions."

"Sounds great. Shoot!" I responded, smiling.

"Alright, first question: Jesus and Jonah . . . are they the same person, or totally different people?"

If that question sounds stupid, you were probably raised in the church.

If you were raised in the faith, it's easy to take for granted the endless dates, names, and doctrines you absorbed by osmosis. You have an undergraduate degree's worth of information just floating around in your brain.

But I bet you also absorbed a lot of bad theology and misguided assumptions that have nothing to do with Jesus or the Bible. Lots of people in the church were taught to fear God like a dictator, judge everyone who is not a part of their denomination, or believe that Christianity is fundamentally bad news because *billions* of people are going to burn in a fiery pit for *all eternity*. When you're raised in the church, you get a lot of good, but you also inherit some baggage.

When people who weren't raised in the church come to Eucharist, they help us understand our faith so much more. They sing enthusiastically, and they actually believe the Good News is good. They get excited about new ideas and call us out when we take old ideas for granted.

One Sunday, I handed out a sheet to a few people who were new to Eucharist and had not been raised in the church. It was called the

"Christianese BS Form": "Whenever I say a word that doesn't make any sense and offer no explanation, write it down and call me out."

At the end of the service, they handed me a sheet full of big words. "What did you mean when you said 'righteous'? When you said 'propitiation'? When you said 'justified'?"

And I . . . didn't know.

So many of us have been raised in such a deeply homogenized subculture that we throw around words and concepts even we don't really understand. It takes an outsider, someone with fresh eyes and a different story, to help us see again.

So often we see the differences among us as something to be minimized, but what if the differences among us aren't something to be erased but something to be celebrated? The Bible describes God's mission as the reconciliation of all things, a master plan to bring every fractured piece of creation back together again. Is it so crazy to think that God is reconciling all things because, at some level, we all actually need one another? Maybe the church needs Katy as much as Katy needs the church.

The Table

The early Christians believed that God was on a grand mission to reconcile all things in heaven and on earth. They also understood that the best way to experience this reconciliation wasn't in a worship service or a public lecture but gathered around the table. They would regularly gather together in celebratory meals where all who were followers of Jesus ate together as a sign of the new family God was forming. Even today, the act of eating with a bunch of strangers can be uncomfortable, but in the ancient world it was downright scandalous. The first-century world had very clear lines about who was allowed to eat with whom: men and women ate at separate tables, a slave would serve at their master's table but never join them, and good Jewish people (like Jesus and his disciples) weren't to be caught dead feasting with anyone who wasn't of their ethnic tribe.

The radical call of the early church wasn't to march or protest or rage against the system. The radical call was for men to do the dishes alongside the women. It was for a Jew to sit next to a Gentile and attempt to make some small talk. It was for a master to pass wine to his slave. These simple acts were a peaceful protest against the divided world, a sign that, despite all the baggage and fear and pain between us, in Christ we are one new family gathered at our Father's table.

This is why the apostle Paul was so insistent that "there is no longer Jew or Greek, there is no longer slave or free, there is no longer male and female; for all of you are one in Christ Jesus." Some churches read that text and believe the best way to be "one in Christ" is to pursue uniformity, ensuring everyone agrees on everything and expresses their faith in the same way. If anyone doesn't line up, they can't enter the family. If anyone changes their mind, they are threatened with excommunication. I understand this impulse—certainly, there are core truths that we have to hold as Christians, and there are ways we are meant to live. But if we only focus on the ways we are called to be similar, we end up with a table that's far too tidy.

The early Christians brought their unique backgrounds and stories to Christ's table and allowed the Holy Spirit to fill them and transform them. But that didn't rid them of their embodied experiences. They continued to be different from one another, even while being pulled into a larger story. God, it seems, is interested in a unity that is deeper than uniformity, a church that is made up of radically different people from every type of background who, at the table, become an awkward and glorious vision of a whole new family.

Part of Our Body

Raised Mormon, Lindsey has two master's degrees in divinity, is very tall, very queer, on the autism spectrum, and uses *they/them* pronouns, which I will honor in this chapter. Lindsey is also our card-carrying Anglican. When Lindsey and I first met up for coffee, they spent thirty minutes grilling me on our liturgy: "Do you use incense? Do you follow the old or new Book of Common Prayer? Do you have a bishop?" My answers were, "No," "No," and "Only a fake one." Lots of people think we are a pretty liturgical church, but they tend to be those raised in unceremonious congregations. To anyone with an ounce of high church in their blood, we are mongrels.

Lindsey asked about how we practice Communion in our church. "Is it real presence or just a metaphor?" they asked me, fumbling over coffee. Their whole adult life, they had been taught that the bread and wine are the physical manifestation of Jesus—the actual body and blood of Christ—and they should be treated with the utmost respect. I went on to describe the hot mess that is the Eucharist Communion table, explaining how kids and adults come forward and pass bits of bread to one another in a circle.

"Oh," Lindsey shook their head. "I don't like that!"

"Lindsey," I laughed, "I don't think you're going to like Eucharist! It's probably not the place for you."

"You're really not selling me on your church," they responded, a little confused.

"I'm really not trying to sell you on it," I replied. "I don't think you're going to like us!"

That Sunday, Lindsey came to our gathering. When it was time for Communion, they walked forward, eyes wide open and mortified. There were kids dipping the bread—and most of their hand—into the Communion cup. There were dots of red juice sprinkling the altar, and torn bits of the Sacrament had fallen onto the ground under the table. With ninja speed, Lindsey snatched the little piece of Jesus off the floor, rubbed it across the table to absorb the drops, and then popped the dirty crumb into their mouth. When I tell this story to people, they usually laugh; it seems so extreme to most of us. However, to Lindsey this isn't a joke.

Yet, inexplicably, Lindsey continues to worship with us. They sit among a community filled with low-church losers who have to Google what a thurifer is. Lindsey tells me that being a part of Eucharist has been one of the most frustrating—and transformative—experiences of their life.

But it flows both ways: Lindsey has also transformed us. They are a valuable and vital part of Eucharist: writing liturgy, leading prayers, and showing up on Good Friday, ready to read the Tenebrae—which is a second word for you to Google.

Part of our family loves the church and its tradition. They remind us just how deep and beautiful this faith is.

And there's Jasmine, who loves her church but literally never comes on Sunday. She'll tell others about Eucharist and will show up to every dinner party or camping trip, but for some reason she just can't do the weekly church thing. However, when we needed to raise fifteen thousand dollars to sponsor a refugee, she was on it. She hosted the meetings, researched our options, and coordinated a toilet-paper drive that sold thousands of triple-ply rolls. She'd even come on Sunday to update the community on the fundraising process. Then she'd walk out halfway through the sermon.

Part of our family doesn't show up on Sunday. But they'll lead the charge when it's time to get our hands dirty.

One Sunday, a woman told me that she had been discussing her back pain with two young people in our church. Midconversation, they stopped everything, laid hands on her, and asked God for immediate healing. "See, that's why I need charismatic Christians in my church," she said, wiping tears from her eyes. "My liberal friends would never spontaneously pray aloud for me like that."

Part of our family is quick to pray. They keep us bold and expectant.

One Sunday, I asked a visitor how she had heard about our church. She told me that she had met someone from our community in the psych ward on suicide watch and that they had become good friends. Her friend had then invited her to come to church on Sunday.

Part of our family struggles with mental health. They keep us gritty and honest.

One Sunday, I was breaking bread in front of the congregation with people all around, gathered in a large horseshoe. "On the night he was betrayed, Christ took bread"—I lifted the loaf high in the air—"and after giving thanks, he broke it, saying, 'This is my body, broken for you.'" And in a loud, clear voice, Riley, who is two years old, yelled out, "No, that's *my body!*" And the whole room exploded in laughter.

Part of our family is toddling. They help us to not take ourselves too seriously.

Part of our family is married. They practice love together for the sake of the community.

Part of our family is single. They strengthen the bonds of friendship.

Part of our family is contemplative. They model how to listen.

Part of our family is faith-filled. They urge us to keep hope alive.

Part of our family is doubting. They remind us that skepticism has its place.

Part of our family has immigrated. They carry in their bodies and culture a different side of the Imago Dei.

Part of our family is queer. They remind us that God is found uniquely among those who don't fit neatly into our societal boxes.

Part of our family is building its career. They teach us about the importance of work and hustle.

Part of our family is retired. They remind us that there is life after work.

And each part is vital and valuable.

No church expression is perfect at this. There are still so many cultures and backgrounds missing from our congregation. But the church calls us into life together. Not to be some perfect beacon of diversity but to celebrate the differences that are *already* present. She puts us on a team with people we would never select in a schoolyard pick and invites us to name and celebrate our differences.

God's family is anything but uniform.

But she is, and is becoming, united.

What Kind of Table?

So if we are God's diverse family, called to eat together, what sort of table are we sitting at?

Restaurants offer a predictable experience. You know you can show up and order something off the menu, and it will be delivered right to your table. The price is laid out, the expectations are clear, and you know what you're getting. Restaurants value order and structure, and any young parent will tell you that bringing a crying baby or a restless toddler is taboo.

Restaurants usually feature one type of food without much diversity. In most North American establishments, when you dine with friends, you typically order your own individual item instead of sharing a large dish. The waiter delivers to each person exactly what they want. There are clear lines between who is serving and who is being served. My favorite restaurant moment is after the meal, when you're staring at the war zone of dirty dishes and used napkins, and then you just stand up and walk away. It's glorious.

But following that moment of bliss is the realization that you have to pay for the meal, which doesn't feel so good now that you're no longer hungry. Restaurants are economic spaces that are happy to serve and feed you, provided you have the means to pay your way. If you don't like the meal, you can send it back to the kitchen, or if you're feeling passive aggressive, give it a one-star review online. If the menu changes or you have a bad experience, you never have to return; you have no allegiance to the business. Staff follow a dress code, meals look presentable, and everything is on brand.

Restaurants are uniform.

Some churches are like restaurants. They offer a product for you to consume in exchange for money (or tithes). They serve up religious goods for consumption, with a five-star rating online and a solid social media presence. That's one kind of table. But there's another way to eat together, a festive meal celebrated by families and churches since the dawn of time: the potluck. Potlucks are anything but predictable. You might have lots of food, or you might be a little short. There's a chance you'll end up with too much of the same thing. My friend once threw a potluck for fifteen people and everybody brought meatballs. At a potluck, everyone brings what they can. There's the ambitious mother who bakes three homemade meat pies and the college student who brings rolled bologna. Some people forget to bring anything at all, and they are still welcome. Some of the food is familiar but some of it is foreign, the spices and scents exotic and unknown. There are dishes you like and some you don't, but you want to try a little of everything.

After a potluck, people roll up their sleeves, wash dishes together in a gigantic kitchen sink, and try to sort out whose Tupperware is left over. Potlucks flatten out power hierarchies: everyone is a servant and everyone is served. A good potluck brings with it the full flavor and culture of everyone present; the more diverse the group, the better the meal. If even one person is missing from the potluck, the whole thing changes. Everyone has a role to play in making the meal what it is. Even the children are invited to run around and play. There's a chance they'll try to eat something off your plate even if they don't know you. People dress in their own unique style, the cutlery doesn't match, and the tasting notes clash. Potlucks suck at uniformity. But when everyone is together around the table, sharing a meal, it's clear there is unity.

Jesus speaks often of the kingdom of God, which is his way of describing God's dream for creation. Despite corruption, violence, and evil, Jesus insists that God's kingdom is breaking into the world if only his listeners will have eyes to see. To help wake them up to God's reality, he points to ordinary things around them and says, "The kingdom of God is like that." It's like a mustard seed, starting small and becoming large and disruptive, or, like yeast in dough, it spreads quickly and expands. In a similar way, I want to suggest that the kingdom of God is like a potluck: diverse, participatory, messy, and beautiful. If the church is meant to be the place that most clearly reflects God's kingdom on earth, we should commit ourselves to that kind of table and stop trying to be a five-star restaurant.

At the risk of overstretching the metaphor, what can you bring to the potluck of your church? What sort of meal do you bring when you walk into your community? Do you bring comfort food, sitting with those who need a listening ear? Do you bring some Southern hospitality, welcoming those who are new? Or do you bring something energizing and high in protein, motivating your community to work for justice and peace? Are you an organizer, helping to schedule the meal, or are you in the dish pit, humbly serving behind the scenes? Think about your gifts and personality, the person God has uniquely made you to be, and consider how you might best serve the potluck by bringing what you have.

Or perhaps you're someone who used to be really involved in the potluck, but at a certain point, the whole thing beat you down. Maybe others didn't understand or appreciate what you brought to the table, or you felt unnoticed or undervalued, and so over time you pulled back, little by little, until you were sitting alone at your own table. If that's where you find yourself, I want you to know it's okay. Life in community is vulnerable and difficult work, and sometimes a bit of space and distance can aid the process of healing. But when you've taken the time you need and been able to catch your breath, I also want to humbly invite you to step back into the potluck. And here's why: you have something crucial to offer. Without your participation, the meal will never be all that it can be. And besides, none of us were meant to eat alone.

Our First Hamilton Christmas

A few years ago, Canada received an influx of Syrian refugees, many of whom ended up in our city. A lot of people in our community are deeply involved in the refugee crisis and wanted to find a way for our church to engage with these new arrivals. "What if we hosted a huge Christmas party?" one young woman said to her church pals, feeling particularly ambitious. "Do you think new arrivals would come to that?" The team jumped into action, renting out a hall, stuffing Christmas bags full of toys, and inviting all their refugee friends. The night of the party, Eucharites drove around the city, squeezing families into minivans. Each family brought towering trays of traditional Syrian dishes. Our people showed up with significantly less-interesting food.

They were Muslim refugees who had fled from Syria and spoke no English. We were mostly Canadian hipsters who spoke only English and were really into Jesus.

It should have been a disaster.

The food spanned the globe, spilling over the edge of our plates. People sat at tables attempting to converse, leaning heavily on a few translators and some free smartphone apps. The kids came forward for presents, and Eucharist musicians played Christmas carols that we danced to.

After the meal, as we packed up tables and chairs, one of the Syrian elders came up and gave me a great big bear hug before pointing to his phone. He had a YouTube video ready to go, the title of which was completely unreadable to me. He then pointed to the speaker system and back to the phone. We plugged in the device and he pressed Play. Loud, unrecognizable music blasted through the speakers, and the Syrians began to clap. They formed a circle, and the elder started spinning in the middle. One of our translators ran over and told me they were blessing us with a traditional Syrian dance. Our whole church watched, clapping to the rhythm, as they moved through the room, hands waving in the air.

Then one of the Syrians grabbed my arm and pulled me into the circle. Another pulled in an onlooker and before long, the dance was filling the entire hall—dozens of people moving in a circle together, each of us trying to kick our feet and clap our hands at just the right moment.

Everyone linked arms and continued to spin, and I couldn't believe what I was witnessing. There was a college student linked to a refugee mother, who was spinning with her arms joined to a charismatic Christian. Her son was twirling in the middle, holding hands with three brown children. There was a sixty-year-old retired schoolteacher and a dad with a twin on each arm. There was a nurse next to a young mother wearing a hijab, who was next to a lesbian couple. Across from them, an older man shuffled with his walker alongside the atheist who keeps coming to church, and in the middle of the circle, a Muslim elder led the Christian community in a dance.

All of us were smiling and laughing, kicking our feet and running out of breath. When the song ended, everyone cheered at the top of their lungs, the kids spun and clapped, and with tears in our eyes, we took in the variety of colors and accents, smiles and scents. I wanted to yell out to everyone at the top of my lungs, "*How is this happening?*"

But I already knew how.

The kingdom of God is like a potluck.

8 THE MOST HONEST PLACE IN TOWN

As Eucharist began to find her identity, we had to shift our focus in a few ways. While our first two buildings had been on the east end of downtown, we realized as the congregation formed that not everyone was coming from the same east-end neighborhood. It's not like they were driving in from forty-five minutes away; everyone lived within a relatively small stretch of the city core, and most people could still bike on a Sunday. But the image of the whole community traveling one direction to our Sunday gathering felt lopsided. I had this nagging voice in my head insisting that if we could just shift our location to the center of the city, everyone would be able to move inward on Sunday, and balance would be restored on some cosmic level. One could argue it was a bad idea to upend the barely functional scaffolding of a church community only to reposition it two miles down the road, but I'm a little obsessive.

Because Eucharist met in the afternoon, I typically had Sunday mornings free, which gave me time to walk the neighborhood, go for brunch, or frantically finish the slideshow that really should have been done by Thursday. On one such walk, I passed a beautiful and historically significant church building that was right in the heart of downtown. An ornate sign proudly displayed their very classic church name. For the sake of this story, we'll call them "St. Barnabas."

It was nearly noon and their service must have already ended, but the door was still wide open. I tiptoed in like a burglar. The sanctuary was stunning: dark wood met lavish red carpets with stained glass in every direction, which preached the gospel in a way words never could. I walked slowly down the aisle, taking in the history and grandeur of the room, before a shaky voice spoke from the shadows and I nearly jumped out of my skin: "Do you want to join us for tea?" asked an old woman who had just reentered the sanctuary. I followed her down a decorated hallway, past large paintings of previous ministers and framed newspaper articles about the building, which dated back to 1860. By the end of tea-time, I had met the pastor and a few members of their council. St. Barnabas was filled with lovely old saints, but after a decades-long decline, they were down to a few dozen on a Sunday. We were young and growing, looking for a central location and a congregation to build a relationship with. It seemed like we had a lot to offer each other. A few months later, Eucharist packed up a U-Haul and moved into one of the most extravagant buildings in the city, located at the very center of everything.

Every Sunday, we unloaded our sound gear and began the intense process of making that ancient space feel like home for a bunch of disheveled twentysomethings. We set up speakers and amps, put our large sound board across two rows of pews, and built a custom projection screen out of PVC piping and tablecloths. The sanctuary was so large we feared everyone would end up sitting in their own pew, so we hung a massive curtain that cut the room in half and forced people to sit together. We used candles and spotlights to set the mood. After Communion, the congregation sprawled across the front of the sanctuary. Some sat on the stairs that led up to the pulpit, and others perched on the backs of the pews while the band jammed away on their xylophones and guitars. The kids loved being in such a weird building and would run up and down the aisles, screaming. One Sunday, we gathered all the pew cushions together and used them to build a giant pillow fort. I promised the kids that someday soon we'd all bring blankets from home, hang them from the balcony, and create the biggest fort this building had *ever* seen.

The people connecting with our church were so unlike the room we gathered in. One week, a girl walked into church carrying her skateboard and wearing a bikini. In the middle of the service, she walked down the aisle, toward the pulpit, across the sanctuary, past the person giving announcements, through the antique door, and poof: she was gone. Like a really weird angel. The building wasn't even near a beach.

Despite how it sounds, our church wasn't *trying* to be weird or unique. We were trying to be authentic. Like FT in Toronto, the people who had gathered together to become Eucharist were now organically expressing themselves. It turned out they were community-minded, wildly creative, and occasionally in bathing suits. But whatever Eucharist was becoming was way more interesting when amplified by the beautiful, historic sanctuary that now housed our Sunday gatherings. I constantly found myself asking, "How are *these* things happening in *this* space?"

Keep It Real

The more genuine our church became, the more intriguing we were to those around us. A few months into meeting at St. Barnabas, our city's newspaper gave us a front-page article, titled (get ready to cringe): "Church of the Young and Hip." It was pretty awkward and featured some embarrassing lines, including:

"Kevin stands at the counter of Cannon Coffee Co., ordering waffles. 'Afternoon service is the bomb,' he says."

Oh yes, it's "the bomb." Church is a real *groovy* place.

Choice quote aside, the article did a pretty good job articulating what we were trying to do. It explored how young congregations were trying to create a more honest church, one that was rooted to the past but able to express itself in ways that felt genuine and unfabricated. That had become a high value for us. People in our community needed to be able to say what they were actually thinking. They had to be honest about who they were and what they were experiencing. We didn't want to pretend we were a church with all the answers or attempt to cover up our imperfections. Whatever church was meant to be, it had to be *real*.

I know that words like *real* and *authentic* are now among the worst Christian clichés, but I still think they describe something vitally important. Every day, social media influencers try to convince me that we are in some sort of relationship and that if we are really friends, I should purchase whatever new product they are hawking. According to *Forbes* magazine, experts believe that in our digital world, the average person sees up to ten thousand advertisements a day. My generation has been marketed to since the day we were born, and we're really good at sniffing it out. We know when someone's lying. So don't try to sell us your happy-clappy church when the world is on fire; don't sell us your big smiles when we all know someone fighting cancer. Don't slap Jesus's name on positive thinking and call it Christianity.

Call it *being authentic* or *real* or *genuine* or whatever language you want to use. But I'll put it as bluntly as I can: if we're going to be the church together, we have to cut the BS.

Sad Church

When it comes to being BS-free, Hebrew poetry is an excellent companion. Take the Psalms, for example. The Psalms are a collection of songs and poetry found in the middle of the Hebrew Scriptures (what many Christians call the Old Testament), and they are layered and complex. While most have an element of hope in them, the majority are also drenched in sadness and grief. They are less "Jesus is my boyfriend" and more "darkness is my closest friend." Naturally, this leads to many Christians being quite selective about which Psalms they read in church and results in some pretty creative editing around the messy parts. But the poets knew that we could not have light without dark, hope without despair, or faith without doubt. They made room for the full spectrum of human emotion.

As we settled into St. Barnabas, we wanted to become as authentic as the psalmists.

We sang songs of lament, talked openly about our struggles, and began hosting the "Wake for a Righteous Man." This is our Good Friday event, in which the congregation dresses in black, gathers late in the evening, and grieves the death of Jesus. The room is bathed in candlelight, and all mirrors are draped with black fabric. Guests bring funeral food (the Canadian staple, Nanaimo bars, and triangle sandwiches) and lots of wine. People make small talk and more or less embrace the discomfort that comes with a funeral. Over the course of the evening, a few of the guests go up to the microphone and read a eulogy they've written from the perspective of someone who knew Jesus. This might be a well-known character in the Bible who interacted with Jesus (like Peter or Martha), an obscure biblical character (like Pontius Pilate's wife), or one who is entirely fictitious (perhaps someone who witnessed the crucifixion firsthand). After giving their speech about the deceased, they raise their glass "to a righteous man." The room clinks glasses in a toast, the classical music swells back up, and small talk resumes.

I don't police what those giving the speech say or which character they pick. We only have two rules: (1) Be candid about how your character feels. (2) Don't know the future.

The speakers aren't allowed to say, ". . . but I know he will rise in three days," because those grieving the death of Jesus didn't know what would happen next. They didn't have any spoilers. Sometimes we need to put ourselves in their sandals and feel what they might have felt. We've now hosted the Wake for over five years, and it's become one of our favorite events. What struck me recently was that at least half our guests are now visitors from other church communities. When I ask these guests why they've joined us, I always hear some variation of the same thing: "It's real."

Over the years, all of this authenticity gave us a bit of a reputation. "Do you know what people are calling us?" someone in the congregation asked me one Sunday. "They're calling us *sad church*!"

"Oh no," I responded, "is that bad?"

"Are you kidding? I love that we're sad church!" she said, laughing. "There are so many happy churches out there; somebody needs to embrace the tears."

I'm still not sure exactly what kind of church we are. We aren't always happy, but I don't think we're particularly depressed. I hope we're living out the words of theologian Walter Brueggemann, when he says:

"Churches should be the most honest place in town, not the happiest place in town."

Sticky Notes

In our first year of meeting at St. Barnabas, we made a few mistakes. The kids had marked up their decorative guest book (beneath beautiful cursive handwriting were two poorly spaced scribbles: "E LL io T" and "AN n a c LA I rA"). One large man in our church sat down and accidentally popped off the back of an old pew. And we struggled to properly lock the very complicated antique doors. We were trying our best to honor the space, but there was a fairly steep learning curve.

One Saturday, we rented St. Barnabas's kitchen to host our first "thank you for serving in your church" appreciation breakfast. The whole community showed up. I flipped pancakes while our leadership team set up tables and sizzled the minisausages. Everyone was laughing and chatting when the door to the back hall flew open and Agnes marched into the hall. Agnes was a fiery Scottish woman with a very short fuse. She stormed into the kitchen, grabbed me by the arm, waved her finger in my face, and shouted at me: "You people don't know how to listen!" Agnes was convinced we hadn't booked the space for our meal. She was red in the face with beaded sweat on her brow as she stood directly in front of me and yelled, "*You people are ruining this building!*" Then she pivoted on a dime and stormed out of the hall. The whole church was wide-eyed and uncertain of what to do next. I ran off to compose myself and took deep breaths in the side room, but it was useless. I felt like a kid again, slapped on the wrist and humiliated in front of everyone.

The following Sunday, I arrived at St. Barnabas with the setup team, ready to pull out the speakers, build our makeshift PVC screen, and hang the curtain. As we passed through the old door into the foyer, I noticed a bright yellow sticky note on its dark wood frame, but there was no message written on it. There was a second yellow square stuck on the handrail in the hallway and a third on the door to the sanctuary. Finally, we walked into the sanctuary and froze in place—there were sticky notes *everywhere*: on the backs of pews, crawling up pillars, and speckled on walls. There was one in the nave, up at least fifteen feet high. It was like a biblical plague of sticky notes had descended upon us. Finally, at the front of the sanctuary where we set up our band was one final note. Written on it in black Sharpie: "EVERY YELLOW STICKY NOTE IS A SCRATCH THAT YOU PEOPLE PUT IN THIS BUILDING."

I don't know how they were certain of which marks we'd made or how we possibly damaged a surface fifteen feet in the air, but there was no use in fighting about it. I took pictures of the sticky notes, and we debated covering everything we owned in bubble wrap. Over the following month, there was no communication, and it felt like things were finally going to settle. But when I popped into the building on my way to a New Year's Eve party, sitting on the front-hall table was a letter. The envelope's beautiful hand-writing read, "Kevin Makins, Eucharist Church." I sat down, read the letter, and felt my heart sink like a stone in the sea. Our lease had been terminated. We were being kicked out of the building.

We had three weeks to find a new space, pack our things, and be gone.

Wilderness Sunday

I was devastated and embarrassed. After all, it was my stupid idea to move across town into a grandiose Gothic sanctuary. I remember driving away from the building, my head spinning with questions: *What will people think when they find out? What if they don't trust me anymore? What if everyone gives up on our church?*

And then I had a horrible idea: What if I covered the whole thing up? I didn't need to *lie* to the community; I could just bend the details. I could tell them that the space wasn't working out for either party. It could be a mutual breakup. *Come to think of it,* I thought, *maybe I do sense God calling us in a different direction.* It wasn't just about my ego. The congregation didn't deserve to feel this rejection. Telling them we were kicked out would only cause unnecessary turmoil. There had to be some way to move out of St. Barnabas without losing all credibility.

While all this was happening, I was auditing a class in Toronto with Brian Walsh. Brian and his wife, Sylvia, were farmer-theologians whose work had deeply impacted many of us at Eucharist. During one of our classes, Brian began to speak about the wilderness in Scripture and how it is a place of struggle and disorientation where nothing makes sense anymore. The wilderness is where God's people are tried and tested. It reveals who they really are. Hearing about the wilderness was the last confirmation that there was no way to spin getting kicked out of St. Barnabas. To do so would be to betray the authenticity of Eucharist. We weren't going to leave the space as winners. There would be no victory march. The grace of God would only reach us if we leaned in to what we had been learning for the past year: we needed to name what was happening, speak openly about how it felt, and not try to wrap it up with a bow.

We needed to be honest.

Brian and Sylvia volunteered to join us on our last Sunday at St. Barnabas and brought with them a stack of cardboard and a handful of markers. "The wilderness is a place of incredible opportunity and growth," Sylvia said to our community, "and simultaneously a place of great difficulty and struggle."

Sylvia invited some volunteers forward and gave them cardboard and a marker. "So, let's do an exercise together," she said to the room. "Which characters from the biblical story spend time in the wilderness?" There was a brief moment of silence before one brave soul shouted out, "Abraham!"

"Yes!" she replied enthusiastically. "Abraham was called by God to leave his home—his security and provision—and to head toward a promised land." Sylvia then asked one of the volunteers to draw a picture of Abraham from memory. "Maybe give him a little staff or a sheep or something?" she encouraged the artist, before turning back to the room. "Who else was in the wilderness?"

"Jacob," said someone in the front row.

"Yes! Jacob wrestled with an angel and left with a blessing, but also a limp." Another artist drew a picture of a stumbling Jacob.

"Who else was in the wilderness?" Sylvia asked. Now the room had warmed up: "Elijah," shouted someone in the back. "John the Baptist," said another, followed by "Hagar." On and on we went until we had over a dozen sheets of cardboard covered in illustrated Bible characters. They carried fluffy sheep and wooden sticks, and one was surrounded by hungry lions while another was fed by ravens. A few of them were on fire or headless. After putting all the characters in chronological order, Sylvia asked, "What proportion of the biblical story do we have in the wilderness?"

Our eyes scanned left to right and back again, and we saw every key person in the biblical story.

"We wouldn't have a story if we didn't have the wilderness." Sylvia pointed out that, while Eucharist was entering into the wilderness, St. Barnabas had been there for much longer. They had witnessed congregational decline and a loss of cultural influence while being stuck with an expensive and impossible-to-maintain building, which drained them of resources. Was it any surprise that the added discomfort of our young congregation finally broke the camel's back? I had hoped they would be able to respond to these challenges with courage and imagination. I wanted St. Barnabas to welcome a young church and her chaos, but after 150 years of stability, how would I feel if I was of the generation that witnessed members die off and watched youth walk away?

There's a good chance I'd also cling to the little bit of security I had left.

When Brian got up to close out the sermon, he told us about how, decades earlier, he had been a part of a young church plant, which had also been kicked out of an older congregation's building. He talked about how his anger eventually turned into grace and how the church that booted him is now a flourishing community again. That needed to be our hope for St. Barnabas. They were on their own wilderness journey, and we had to pray they would reach their promised land.

Keeping a Promise

Of all the wilderness stories in Scripture, the central one is of the Israelites, who longed for the promised land after being freed from their slavery in Egypt. For forty years, they wandered in the desert, continuing to praise God while also being honest about their less-than-ideal living arrangements. Whenever they set up camp, they would also construct a large tent, called a tabernacle, in which they would eat, worship, and recognize God's presence with them in the wild. I always visualized the tabernacle as an awesome blanket fort—the biggest you'd ever seen.

Which reminded me of a promise I had made to the kids of our church, one I intended to keep.

After Sylvia and Brian's sermon, we walked into the back hall. The space had been turned into an epic pillow fort. Over our heads were dozens of bedsheets, each one donated by members of our congregation. They had been strung together into a large canopy that hung over our heads. Twinkling lights ran between the seams, and pillows littered the floor. We enjoyed our last meal at St. Barnabas, stuffing our faces and dancing with the kids. We knew the next day, we'd pack up our blanket fort—our tabernacle—and head into the unknown.

Yes, being kicked out of the building sucked, and being honest about it didn't make it any less painful. But it also felt really good. We didn't need to put on fake smiles or pretend everything was okay. We had nothing to hide. Whatever happened next, we were in this adventure together: honest, open, and ready to wrestle whatever obstacles we met in the wilderness.

We might walk away with a blessing, but we'd also leave with a brutal limp.

9 A PARTICULAR GLORY

Children's books, clunky old speakers, and strange art projects packed up, we drove the moving truck a whole mile down the road to our fourth temporary location at First Christian Reformed Church. With such short notice, we desperately needed a warm space to meet through the winter but didn't want to commit to a new home base with only one month to search. Another church in our local TrueCity network graciously welcomed us into their place, and their setup was way nicer than the living arrangements we were used to. The sanctuary had two opulent drop-down projector screens, individual classrooms for each age group of kids, even accessible ramps for walkers (occasionally present at our gatherings) and strollers (overwhelmingly present at our gatherings). It definitely felt like we were kids moving back in with our parents after failing to launch.

One of the people helping us move was Jake, who, after twenty-three years of seeing spirituality as an open field, was hesitantly considering the front door of our church. A

Hamiltonian through and through, Jake was raised by a working-class father after being taken away from his drug-addicted mother. Church wasn't ever on his Sunday radar. Instead, his Sundays had consisted of a sacred ritual: drinking beer and cheering for the Jets. And yet, throughout his life, Jake had a keen sense of the "something more" that hummed just below the surface of daily life. He had bumped up against it when, as a comedian, the room got lost in the intoxicating joy of laughter. Drugs, alcohol, and hookups brought moments of transcendence, but they were fleeting at best. He continued his quest for enlightenment by learning to survive off kale and sprouts as a vegan, and he eventually got into daily yoga. But despite an openness to any and all religions and worldviews, he still felt spiritually hungry inside. There was no particular path he could walk on to help him experience the glory of God, which was all around him.

Also moving old art projects through the basement was Eric.

If Jake was raised in an open field, Eric experienced a narrow hallway. Raised in a very conservative branch of the church, he was given a thorough religious education through Christian school, chapel services, midweek Bible study, and church twice on Sundays. Throughout high school and college, this expression worked well for Eric, giving him a language of prayer, a community to participate in, and a well-worn path on which to walk toward God. But as he entered into adulthood, the tradition he was given no longer fit comfortably. It felt too tight and rigid, a corset that kept him from breathing in the fresh air of the Spirit. When he eventually met people outside of his tribe, he discovered they weren't evil. Some of them were actually far healthier than the people he was raised around. The clear lines between "us" and "them" began to blur and fade as he asked the hard questions he had always been given easy answers to: questions about the Bible and church, judgment and truth. Though it felt safer to stay within the particulars he had been handed, doing so could no longer satisfy his spiritual hunger. A larger understanding of God was pulling him forward.

These two people came into our community from opposite backgrounds: one wandered through a vague universal spiritualism, in which the divine was located everywhere; the other was steeped in a particular religious expression, which saw the divine as residing exclusively within itself. Yet each of them had come up against the limitations of their respective backgrounds and felt a desire to step beyond them. When this happens, it can feel scary, like everything we know is falling apart.

But things need to fall apart if they are going to be put back together again.

Glory

Wandering through the wilderness, the Israelites had learned to see God all around them. They'd encountered the goodness of God as he fed them with bread from heaven and led them by a pillar of cloud. As mentioned in the last chapter, every time they stopped, they set up a tabernacle under which they worshiped. This would have looked similar to a large tent. In fact, the word *tabernacle* is often translated simply as "tent." Of course, as many of us know, setting up a tent is super annoying, so when the Israelites have settled their new land, they eventually get to work constructing a particular place where God can dwell permanently: the temple. Upon its completion, the Israelites hold a dedication ceremony. The cloud of God's glory overwhelms the room, and all the people fall flat on their faces in fear and reverence.

They agree this will be the particular place where they will meet with God.

The Bible is surprisingly ambivalent when it comes to the temple. Worshiping in one specific place may help them concretely engage with God's glory, but it also brings with it certain risks. The people might assume that the universal God can *only* be found in the "sanctioned" place. More dangerous still, they may attempt to tame the wild fire, trying to *use it* instead of being *led by it*.

Of course this is what happens. The Israelites act like all the other nations and use their "god" for power and wealth. One of the nations they buddy up with, Babylon, eventually turns on Israel, enslaves the people, and destroys their sacred places. As the dark smoke of the burning temple vanishes into the air, so does the glory of God. It isn't until seventy years later that a few of the Israelite captives are permitted to go back to the destroyed city and rebuild the temple. But when they finally dedicate the restored temple, there is no miraculous moment. God doesn't appear in a blaze of fire. They have rebuilt the temple, but things can't just go back to the way they had been before.

God has hidden his glory from them.

The Power of *No*

Never underestimate the impact of a good coffee shop. A woman in our church had started a café down the street from our rental building, which is how she first met Jake, who had just returned from a failed yoga trip to India. "I'm just too competitive for yoga," he shouted, waving his hands and working out a comedy bit. "I need some enlightenment that doesn't depend on my ability to get both my legs over my head."

She laughed and responded, "It sounds like you're describing grace. Jesus was pretty into that!" Then she paused for a moment before deciding to just go for it: "You should come to my church sometime. It's sort of crappy, but we like it."

Eric first came to Eucharist when, in a moment of pure rebellion, he dated someone outside of his family's denomination. She was a lovely young woman who deeply loved Jesus, but in his tradition, it was as scandalous as Romeo and Juliet. She brought him to one of our services, which he found both appealing and appalling. After the sermon, he cornered me and tried to pin down our doctrine. When I told him we don't prescribe theological answers for most nonessential beliefs but instead let people wrestle through the questions together, I thought he'd never come back again. But Eric continued to show up and get involved in the community, even after he and Juliet broke up. He started to notice how God was meeting him in unexpected places—through nature and art, loud music venues, and late-night bike rides. Eric was taking apart his faith and slowly putting it back together again, but this time, it wasn't built on the certainty of his theological perspectives or denominational affiliation. God was bigger than all that. Eric's reconstructed faith was as much about the mystery as it was about the answers.

Jake found the openness of our congregation a natural fit but was caught off guard by what, to him, seemed like such a narrow expression of spirituality. We sang praise songs, read the Bible, and talked about Jesus . . . a lot. Jake later told me his whole spiritual life had been about exploring spaces without doctrine, where simply having a spiritual thought was applauded, even if all his ideas were vague and contradicting. When someone at Eucharist asked him a question about his beliefs, Jake spouted off some opinion about the universe and waited for an approving statement like, "Yeah, man, it's just whatever works for you."

Instead, the person he was talking to said, "I disagree." For the first time, his ideas were challenged, and he was forced to question his thoughts and articulate what he actually believed about God. For someone raised with a vague, universal idea of faith, the particularity of that *no* meant more than any *yes*.

Eric and Jake were encountering God from two different directions, but that didn't mean they weren't witnessing the same glory.

Mountaintop

It's been five hundred years since the temple was rebuilt, and while life has carried on, many Israelites still anticipate the day when the glory of God will again be revealed in blinding light. Around this time, an unconventional teacher is traveling from city to city, preaching about God's reality and gathering a ragtag pack of disciples. Among his followers are three that he is especially invested in: Peter, James, and John.

One evening, Jesus wakes them from sleep and whispers, "Come with me." They follow him in the stillness of night, through the camp and toward the base of a nearby mountain, where he begins his ascent. When they arrive at the summit, Jesus is standing before them, staring out into the distance as the sun begins to rise. Peter watches the shadows creep over the mountaintop but notices they are crawling in different directions. They aren't being lit by the dawn. There is a second source of light. Jesus is radiating, undergoing a transformation, a metamorphosis, before them. As he turns around to face them, they raise their hands to cover their eyes. It's as if the sun, which has been studied and worshiped for all of human history, is just the dim reflection of something far brighter. Suddenly, their bones are responding to the vision, some ancient programming hardwired into them since the dawn of time. And without thought or intent, they fall facedown on the ground, pushing their foreheads into the dirt as hard as they can.

And these good Jewish boys, raised in the story of their people, know what this means: the fire that led their ancestors through the wilderness, which later filled the temple and now has been missing for five hundred years, is back. The glory has returned.

It's dwelling not in a place but in a person.

Gathering courage, Peter looks up from the ground and finds that the light has begun to settle, and two others are talking to Jesus. It's Moses and Elijah! The old heroes of the nation. Peter takes a moment to gather his thoughts: *This is too good an opportunity to waste. How often do you get these three together?* So, in a move so bold and knuckleheaded only Peter could pull it off, he stands to his feet and hesitantly approaches the three: "Lord," he says, hoping to get Jesus's attention, "it's a good thing we are here!" Which is the greatest understatement of all time. Moses, Elijah, and Jesus are just hanging out casually, glowing on a mountain? Yes, it's nice to have been invited. "But let me do one thing," he says, taking a step forward. "Let me build three tents, one for each of you."

Of course, the word *tents* is how we typically translate this story into English. The Greek word could also be translated as *tabernacle*. The kind of tent the Israelites set up in the wilderness as a place for the glory of God to dwell.

Peter sees the glory, and his first instinct is to lock it down in a particular place.

As he is talking, the radiating light begins to flare up again and Peter's whole body buckles. He's back on his face, pressing even harder into the ground this time. Then a voice from heaven booms, like slow rolling thunder, "This is my Son, whom I love. *Listen* to him."

Stop talking, stop planning, stop trying to figure it all out. Listen.

The three disciples are quiet and still, unable to perceive whether it's been two minutes or ten hours. Then, in one of those tender moments of Scripture, they feel a hand on their shoulder. This gives us so much insight into how Jesus feels about his friends. After emanating God's glory, he could, as King, beckon them forward. But instead, Jesus touches them and says, "Do not be afraid." When they look up, both the visitors and the glorious light have faded, and staring down at them is their ordinary, thirty-three-year-old Jewish carpenter friend.

Descending the mountain together, Jesus commands them not to say anything about this until after his death, but Peter can hardly hear the words. He's fixated on every detail of Jesus's face. How can it be that hidden behind those dry lips, just below the pores of his dark skin, the glory of God is on full display? Has it been hiding in plain sight all along? And if that's the case, where else might the glory of God be hiding? In the face of a beggar? In the song of a bird?

Perhaps, after seeing God's glory in one particular person, Peter will be able to notice it everywhere else he goes.

The Universal and the Particular

I find this relationship between the particular and the universal fascinating. Some of us were raised like Eric, taught to see the glory of God in only church-sanctioned places and expressions. There are good things that can come from this narrow perspective. It's easier to form cohesive social groups when you know what you're supposed to believe; you can act quickly when you "know" all the answers about what is right and wrong. But this confidence has a dark shadow because no one group has a monopoly on knowing Christ, and none of us are without our blind spots. Beyond that, if we equate God with our church, tradition, or even our religious expression, we are in danger of doing what the Israelites did: turning the roaring lion into a tame house cat. God will not be locked down. The whole biblical story is about a God who keeps showing up in unexpected places.

Others of us, like Jake, have held a vague universal spirituality. It's good to try to live with open minds and compassion, but in a world with limitless options and opinions, that's rarely enough to keep us rooted. Unable to clearly articulate what is good and what is evil, what is true and what is false, many people become quickly overwhelmed by the abundance of perspectives. They end up like Sandra Bullock's character in *Gravity*: cut off from the satellite that keeps us in orbit and flung into the darkness of space, spinning faster and faster into the infinite void.

There is a trend I've noticed, especially among younger Christians, to leave the particularity of the Christian faith behind in order to pursue loving everyone all the time. The desire to erase the lines that have been drawn between groups of people in order to treat every person as simply a human being comes from really good intentions. But good intentions often fail to work out in concrete action. It's easy to love everyone from a distance, but it can be nearly impossible to love one difficult person you see every Sunday. Lots of my friends drop out of church because they want to meet God in the woods on Sunday morning, and they do . . . for about two weeks. Then they sleep in and watch Netflix. In my experience, most Christians who walk away from the faith end up jumping from one spirituality to another, rotating worldviews like fad diets, never diving deep enough to truly understand or respect any of them.

Here's an illustration maybe you can relate to: When I was a kid, I had to save my money for weeks in order to buy a new CD. After picking up an album, I'd run to my room, sit down with my Discman, put on my oversized headphones, and listen to the whole thing in one sitting. Often, there were tracks I initially disliked, but through repeat listens, I'd find myself loving them. If the album was good, I'd uncover new layers to the music or themes. Those albums became a part of my life. Now, in our age of music streaming, I almost never listen to a full album, and I immediately skip any track that doesn't hook me. But no music impacts me the way it used to. Often, I'm so overwhelmed by options, I don't know what to listen to when I get into the car.

The same is true when it comes to faith. We can skip through a few tracks from a variety of different worldviews, but we may end up failing to properly appreciate or understand any of them. Perhaps, in a culture of instant gratification where we can stream every show and swipe right on endless faces, there is a unique power that comes with being anchored in a community, a tradition, and a sacred text long enough that we're forced to doubt it and question it, to hate it and love it. This doesn't mean we can't ever move on from traditions or communities; we started a new church, so I'm clearly in favor of innovation. But there is wisdom in moving more slowly and more humbly than the culture around us.

So here's my suggestion: we learn to honor the universal by first being faithful to our particular.

For me as a Christian, that means going to church, praying for my enemies, singing hymns, giving generously, confessing the creed, welcoming the stranger, and learning to see God where I've been planted. It's only after I've seen the glory within my limitations that my eyes are trained to see it on a hike in the woods, in a local coffee shop, or in the face of an annoying neighbor. In this way, my Christian faith is like a telescope: it's only by looking through the small eyepiece that I can see the universe.

Being rooted in a particular faith and community is also a much healthier way to build bridges in a deeply divided world. I was once asked to pray at a citywide rally of support after an attack on a mosque in Quebec City. I wasn't asked because I was a generically spiritual, good person. I was asked to pray because I was a Christian pastor. When I, still holding all the distinctions of my faith, stand in a universal love with the Muslim community, who holds different beliefs than mine, *then we are building bridges.*

This is why I am convinced that being a part of the church is so important. She gives us a particular way to experience, live out, and witness to the glory of a God who is beyond our comprehension.

Where the Glory Is

One of the last writings in the Bible is a letter by Peter, who has experienced so much adventure since he met Jesus. Now, as he approaches his execution by the state, he has one last letter to write. As he's reflecting back on his life, he is, of course, going to mention the time he saw Jesus radiating glory on a mountaintop, but as he transitions into the story, he says something subtle and brilliant. He writes, "I think it is right to refresh your memory as long as I live in *the tent of this body.*"

You caught it, right? This brilliant throwback to his own story? When he was young, Peter saw the glory of God as being in *only* one particular place. It was something to be pinned down and guarded on a mountaintop. But now that he is older and has followed Jesus longer, he understands that God's glory is hidden all through creation. Even in him.

He is a tabernacle, a tent, a dwelling place for God's glory. He has become the particular place from which the light will illuminate even the most dreadful darkness.

Christian tradition tells us that the emperor Nero demanded Peter be crucified just as Jesus had been. Convinced he was not worthy to die in the same way as his Lord, Peter insisted the Romans crucify him upside down. Which means that even on that cross, as the blood ran down his inverted body, blinding his eyes and filling his nostrils, there was a light shining in the darkness that could not be overcome. Death did not defeat Jesus, and violence would not have the last word here. For those with eyes trained to see it, there is an invisible glory, even in the greatest suffering.

This same glory would continue to fill tents across the world and throughout millennia, eventually dwelling in a young comedian who had been searching for a particular.

Remember Your Baptism

After a year and a half of hanging around our church family, Jake decided he wanted to follow Jesus and be baptized. It was a cold Sunday in early spring when we filled a metal dunk tank on the front lawn of First Christian Reformed Church, our temporary location. Jake stood up and told his story of faith: how God had called him out of the universal into a particular. And as he told his story, Eric was listening. Over the previous years in our community, Eric had found his faith growing and expanding; he was becoming aware of God in unexpected places. He had longed to express this transformation in some tactile way and had wondered about baptism. But he had already been baptized as an infant by his family and, while he no longer saw God only in the particular church he was raised in, he still wanted to honor them.

So when I asked if anyone else wanted to be baptized, Eric felt paralyzed. Part of him wanted to silently respect his family of origin. The other part wanted to run into the waters and be born again . . . again. But hearing Jake's testimony had reinforced the importance of the foundation he was given. Whether his faith was recognized by his family or not, he was still walking with Jesus, and he was grateful for the narrow hall he had been raised in.

He stayed in his seat and let the moment pass.

But baptism isn't a onetime washing. It's a new way of being. Our pastoral intern, Leshia, who has a real way with words, once called baptism "a vinegar we are pickled into for life." So, after everyone had been dunked, I invited the community to come forward, touch the waters, and "remember your baptism." It was so cold outside that most people were hesitant to get wet at all. A young man near the front ran his hand through the water, and another person solemnly anointed her forehead, but Eric rushed from the back of the crowd, making a beeline to the metal tank. He grabbed onto it with both hands and dunked his entire upper body. The congregation turned toward him in shock, but his eyes were fixed on Jake. With great determination, Eric said to him, "I remember my baptism."

When the church draws in different people, she also connects their stories. Despite hardly knowing one another, Jake and Eric had brought together the universal and the particular, and on that baptism Sunday, we saw that they weren't opposites at all. They danced around one another as beautiful partners.

Of course, that's just what some of us saw.

Others saw these opposites as fundamentally incompatible, worn pieces of fabric which were being pulled in two different directions and couldn't possibly hold together much longer. Soon the seams would tear. To them, it wasn't a question of *if* but *when* Eucharist would rip herself to pieces.

10 NEW CHURCH

When I read memoirs that end with a wedding, my immediate question is always, "Then what happened?" What happened the next week, the next year, and over the next decade? Did love last? Did the couple become cold and bitter? Did a lifetime of disappointment and resentment result in it all falling apart?

And if things did fall apart, how does that change the beautiful story I was invested in?

We were now four years into our life as a church community, still meeting in our temporary fourth location, and things just kept getting more complex. We had a larger budget and rotating volunteer schedules, multiple Sunday school rooms and a leadership team. I had hundreds of unanswered emails and a serious case of emotional fatigue. For years, I had been running off the adrenaline of what God was doing in people's lives, but that, too, had become more complicated.

Back in our first location, the fashion studio, we had been able to watch people encounter God for the first time:

some who had decided to follow Jesus and be baptized or two people who met and fell in love. Some had wrestled for years with addiction issues and then, in our church, finally slayed their dragon. But being in community also meant we'd continued to walk together, even after God did a big thing in someone's life. Years later, we recognized how everyone's story continued to progress, and not always in the expected direction. The person who had found faith might doubt it, the newlywed couple might divorce, or the addict might relapse. The big moments we celebrated were the end of one chapter and the beginning of another. And the new chapter would bring with it new monsters to fight.

Of all the books that neatly tie things up, religious ones have the tidiest bow wrapped around them. They tell stories of churches growing and people coming to faith, but I always want to interrupt with some follow-up questions: "Umm, excuse me . . . did the new convert keep walking with God, or did they walk away two years later? Did she continue to care for her sickly mother? Did the congregation stay that large? Did it become unmanageable? Did the church collapse under the very things that helped her grow?" These are worthwhile questions in light of the string of megachurch scandals that have rocked the evangelical world, especially from many on the Christian bestsellers list.

As a pastor, I'm extra sensitive to this reality because I steward people's stories. I meet with them for coffee and go with them to their immigration hearings, meet with their caseworkers and get weepy phone calls at 1:00 a.m. I have the joy and honor of walking with people through the most difficult struggles of their lives, and when they come out the other side with more love and more joy, and walking closer to God, I want to tell their stories.

And I do.

I might use their story as an illustration in a sermon, interview them on our podcast, or write about them in a blog post. When I share, the whole community celebrates what God has done. And then sometimes, out of nowhere, *they just disappear.* They stop showing up on Sundays and ditch their small group; they don't return my texts and emails and faxes. And I want to scream, "But what about that moment we shared, the positive hearing on your immigration status, the meals the community brought you? Did that mean nothing?" Other times, people continue to hang around but grow cold and stagnant. When they first join us, it's as if they have plugged in to a whole new energy source, but then their spiritual cord gets all bent out of shape, like an old phone charger that can only work if it's leaning at *just* the right angle. They sit in the back row with their arms crossed, simultaneously bored and annoyed by church and God and me.

And then there are the times when some information comes to light that is *so horrible* it retroactively tarnishes all the good stuff that came before it.

I call this the "Cosby Factor."

For example—and I'm just spitballing here—let's say a young person has his life radically changed through your community, and you've been sharing his story for a year, and people have been celebrating it. But then it comes out that, oh, I don't know . . . he was having an affair with the enthusiastic woman who first invited him to church and led him to faith.

Not that anything like that has ever happened to us . . .

What do you do when the "success stories" become the "painful stories"?

How do you continue to love people when you've been hurt?

Not I, Lord

Jesus was well aware of our human propensity to wound one another. When Jesus recognizes his time is running out—that any moment he will be stripped naked and paraded through the streets, insulted and spit on, nailed to a cross and left to bleed dry in the heat of the day—all he wants is one last meal with his disciples. He wants to wash their feet, to pass on his final words, and to make sure that they know how much he loves them. They aren't just disciples or servants doing a master's bidding; they are his friends.

But Jesus also knows what friends do to each other. One of his friends will betray him, handing him over to the authorities to be executed; the others will run away, scattering like cockroaches when the light turns on. Knowing their limits, Jesus says to them, "Where I am going, you cannot come." But Peter, God bless him, isn't convinced. He jumps up from his seat: "Why can't I follow you now?" he says, putting his hand to his sword. "I will lay down my life for you."

And Jesus turns to his dearest friend and speaks the harshest truth to him: "Peter . . . before the morning comes and the rooster crows, you will have denied me three times." We all start off like Peter, insistent that *we* won't let down the people we love. Others might betray their friends, leave them, or deny them, but not good people like *us*. We want to believe that we can truly love one another without truly harming one another.

And, of course, that's just not true.

In the words of C. S. Lewis, "To love at all is to be vulnerable." To love is to risk being hurt.

Hard Times

I'm about to tell you a story that still makes me a little uncomfortable, and I need to remind you that I am both limited by my own recollection of it and stuck in my own bias. Others involved will have their own angle on the event. Please keep all that in mind as you read.

Early on at Eucharist, an eighteen-year-old single mother joined our community. She ended up falling in love with another member of our congregation, a young man who had been left by his wife a few years earlier and had been finding his own footing with us. During their engagement, he was in a near-fatal accident and ended up in the hospital. I was out of town, stuck five hours north, when it happened, but their friends from church jumped in to help them. They went to the hospital and watched her kid, prayed and brought meals. Over the following months, he went through a very challenging recovery process but through it all was able to find some healing. That summer, I performed their wedding ceremony, and it was a jubilant celebration. We danced late into the night, and I remember looking around at all these people who had met because we decided to start a weird church on a Sunday afternoon and thinking about how perfectly things had turned out.

But over the next few months, the couple stopped showing up on Sundays.

I messaged them shortly after and we got together at a small diner downtown. It turned out that we had seen the past few months very differently. I saw their church friends as part of the congregation, caring for them in their trauma. They saw their friends burning out and wondered why the wider church didn't step in. I felt betrayed when they disappeared from the community that had loved them; they felt overlooked during the hardest season of their lives. It was one of those perfect-storm situations: everyone involved wanted to do the right thing, but we were all too ignorant, too burned out, and too hurt to make things right.

They didn't come back to Eucharist, and shortly after, their friends left as well.

This was made worse by the fact that other people were walking away. Some didn't like constantly moving from building to building. Others felt theologically uncomfortable with our welcome of certain people groups. A few said that having an afternoon gathering was nice when they were younger, but now that they had kids of their own, they wanted to go to morning church. Even Sandra and her family, whose renewal-of-vows-and-baptism moment had become such a cultural touchpoint early in our church plant, started attending less and less frequently. Eventually, they dropped out of their small group and stopped showing up on Sundays.

Why Would Anyone Go to Church?

This is when church as a community becomes really difficult. It would be one thing if these were just butts in a pew and all we did was entertain them on Sundays, but we were trying to build an actual family of people who shared life together, and it just seemed to be causing us pain. It was difficult for me as a pastor, but the pain was shared by everyone who had seriously committed themselves to our church. It's so hard when others come and go but you have chosen to stay. You've chosen to be cursed; your heart is an endless revolving door that must remain open and hospitable to whoever walks in next. And you can never feel secure. *Even if* things go amazingly and someone radically matures or comes to faith, it may end up backfiring later.

I was tired of being open. I wanted to board up the door to my heart.

Charcoal Fire

After the arrest, Peter and another disciple head to the courtyard of the high priest, where Jesus is being held. They are almost through the gate when Peter is stopped by a young slave girl. "I recognize you," she says, looking up at his face, illuminated by starlight. "You are one of *his* disciples, aren't you?"

Peter turns his face away and mutters, "I am not." He passes by her quickly and moves toward the radiating heat of a nearby charcoal fire.

Now, it's important to note that, in biblical narrative, anything that isn't crucial is skipped over in a flash. Characters climb and descend whole mountains in half a sentence. But for some reason, the storyteller wants us to remember exactly what Peter is warming himself by. So he uses a unique word in the Greek: *anthrakian*. This word for charcoal fire is used only twice in the whole New Testament.

As Peter rubs his hands together over the coals, attempting to get warm, a commotion forms around him. Another slave walks up,

132

catching sight of Peter's face in the light of the flames. "You are! You are one of his disciples." Peter snaps back, "No, I am not!"

But now a crowd surrounds him, pressing in on all sides, and a lone voice shouts out, "It is him! I saw him in the garden with Jesus. *He cut off my cousin's ear!*"

Finally Peter's eyes break free from the fire, and he turns to speak to everyone at once, shouting, "I swear to God, *I do not know the man!*" And immediately the crowd becomes silent as the cry of the rooster breaks the dawn. Peter throws his hand over his mouth. His eyes fill with tears and his stomach begins to turn. Then he runs out of the courtyard, alone.

And in this painful moment, Peter realizes what all of us eventually realize. We aren't above harming others when we are scared, alone, wounded, or afraid. We're also part of the problem.

Hurt people hurt people.

New Church

It just so happened that, as I was feeling most vulnerable, a new church started just a few blocks over from us downtown. It was also a part of our TrueCity network, and word on the street was that they had started with a small prayer gathering but had grown into a missional movement. It seemed like everyone was talking about how their teaching was so pastoral, their small groups so life-giving, their musicians impeccable. To top it all off, their pastor, Matt, was a friend of mine who happened to have a charming British accent. Whenever I talked to him, I wanted to entrust him with my soul. Apparently, I wasn't the only one who felt this way, as his church became the landing pad for people who had walked away from our community.

One day, I was talking with one of the people who had left Eucharist to join New Church. "It's nice to see some of our old gang there," she said to me with a smile. "It feels like Eucharist was high school and New Church is university!" Ouch.

One baptism Sunday, we were visited by a young man named Blake. He was a local bar owner I'd met years earlier. Every couple of months, we would run into each other on the street and he'd ask if we could go for a walk. He'd chain-smoke and rant about the challenges he was facing, and at the end, I'd pray for him. A few times a year, he'd pop in on a Sunday service, usually after he and whatever girl he was dating at the time broke up. He never came twice in a row, but each time, I could see God was nudging him further down a path. Now he was here again.

That Sunday, a few people from our community told their stories before being baptized, and I threw the invitation out to the congregation: "Is there anyone else here who wants to trust Jesus, die to themselves, and be born again in the water?" I looked into the congregation and saw Blake, eyes filled with tears. He stood to his feet and yelled out, "I need to be baptized!" We took him outside, dunked him below the cold waters, and when we pulled him up, the congregation cheered and hollered. Blake embraced the people he knew around him, drenching them in the same holy water. The next Sunday, Blake was at church, notebook ready, excited to grow in his new faith.

The Sunday after that, he was gone.

That Monday, I called him to ask if he was okay. "Oh yeah, everything is great," he said to me. "I just decided that, since I'm a Christian now, I should have a fresh start with a new community, so I've decided to go to New Church instead."

"*I could have held you under!*" I yelled into the phone before slamming it down.

Eventually I was fed up. *What can possibly be so great about New Church?* I thought to myself as I walked into their Sunday gathering. I sat in the back row and tried to avoid eye contact, but it was hopeless. People came up and greeted me warmly. The prayers were beautiful, and the sermon fed my soul. I was furious. Someone from the New Church leadership team noticed me and ran over. "Kevin!" he said, trying to catch my eye. "I just wanted to say that I attended Eucharist years ago, back when it was in the factory space, and it was so inspiring. It's actually the reason I wanted to help plant New Church! Thank you for being so faithful."

"*Give me my people back!*" I wanted to yell in his sweet face. Instead I responded, "Thank you, we all have our roles to play."

We were no longer the new kid on the block. Our best stories had carried on without us.

If a cat farted into a microphone, we would all just be confused.

Smells Like a Setup

Spoiler alert: Jesus doesn't stay dead. Three days later, he is resurrected, coming back to life and visiting the disciples during dinner. It's got to be a little awkward for Peter, who publicly denied his friend with no opportunity to make things right. But even now, as they share a meal, there is no good opportunity for them to hash things out. When Jesus leaves after dinner, so does Peter's chance to make things right.

A week after the resurrection meal, Peter realizes that, though death might be defeated, there doesn't seem to be any master plan from here. So he rallies a few of the disciples to go fishing, back to where this all began. Apparently, they are out of practice. After a full night's work, they've got nothing to show for their time. The sun is rising as they prepare to head back in, and some guy starts shouting at them from the shore. "Friends!" he yells across the water. "Have you caught any fish?"

Peter feels a flush of embarrassment but can only respond by yelling back, "No!"

The man on the beach begins to laugh, obviously having a bit of fun in this interaction, and then yells, "Try throwing the net on the *other side*."

On the other side . . . are you kidding me? Who is this fishing *genius* who thinks that, after a full night's work, the real problem has been the *side* they threw the net on? But Peter's seen some weird stuff lately. They throw it off the other side, and as soon as the net hits the water, it's filled with fish. The boat is thrown off by the weight, threatening to capsize. Some disciples shout instructions on how to contain the haul, but one of them grabs Peter by the shoulders: "It's Jesus!" And when Peter hears that the man on the shore is his dearest friend, he puts on his cloak and, for the second time, throws himself into the sea to get to Jesus. No miracles this time. No walking on water. But he doesn't need it. He's pushing against the sea with all his strength. Every time his face submerges, he fears that when he comes up for air, Jesus will have disappeared like a mirage on the horizon. But Jesus is still there, guiding him forward. And Peter's not looking away this time.

When he finally gets to shore, he's got sand in his beard and seaweed stuck to his cloak. He catches his breath and gets his first good look at Jesus, who smiles widely, forming familiar laugh lines around his eyes. Jesus points to a nearby rock: "Come and have some breakfast." Only then does Peter notice the small dining area set up, complete with fish, some bread, and . . . a charcoal fire.

A charcoal fire.

Ever feel like God's just setting you up for something?

What Happens in Kansas City . . .

In our TrueCity network of churches in Hamilton, there is a prayer house run by a charismatic woman named Jill Weber. She's the sort of person who will run a prayer room out of the back of a U-Haul truck or lay hands on you to pray for over an hour. Sometimes I think her job is to professionally push me out of my comfort zone.

One day, I got a text.

"Hey, it's Jill. Would you be interested in visiting a church called Navah in Kansas City?" the green text bubble asked. "It would be a prayer pilgrimage with some other Hamilton pastors. Matt from New Church is going." Do I want to pay for a flight . . . to visit one of her strange Holy Spirit churches . . . in Kansas City . . . with the man whose church I am sinfully jealous of?

I slammed my thumbs into the keyboard: "*Nooope!*" But before I hit Send, I Christianed it up a little: "I actually don't feel led by the *Holy Spirit* to do that at this time."

Two days later, I was waiting in line at a local coffee shop when someone behind me said, "*Bro!* Cool tats." Looking around for a rad '90s surfer, I caught the eyes of a young man behind me. He was pointing at the tattoos on my calves, which are completely religious and not at all subtle. He told me that he was a Christian from the southern United States who was in Ontario to get married. After the wedding, he and his new wife were heading off as overseas missionaries. I explained away the religious tattoos by telling him I pastored a church down the street called Eucharist. Then we said goodbye, and I took my coffee to the patio.

Twenty minutes later, the same guy sat down at my table. "Dude, I went on your website and your church seems *awesome!*" he said, still sending out some serious surfer vibes. "It really reminds me of this church in Kansas City called Navah. Have you heard of it?"

I froze. Eyes bugging out in front of me. "What did you just say?" I asked.

"I *know*, right? It's a weird name," he said, reaching for my pen. Then he wrote in my notebook: "NAVAH. KANSAS CITY." "Bro, I really think you'd dig these people," he said, standing up from our table. "If you ever get the chance, you should *totally* go check them out." And then he unfurled his hidden angel wings and surfed off to heaven.

Kidding. He just waved goodbye and walked off, using his legs.

Now, I'm a natural skeptic who will look for every reason to dismiss a coincidence, but in this case even *I* knew something weird was happening, and I knew what I had to do.

But seriously, do you ever feel like God is just *setting you up*?

Peter knew that feeling, sitting next to the sea by a charcoal fire, just waiting for Jesus to ask him about the denial throughout the whole meal. But it wasn't until the meal was finished and the others were busy doing dishes that he was finally alone with his friend. That's when Jesus asked him an important question, one that would finally bring to light all that had been haunting him.

The first two days of our trip, I felt like Peter—just waiting for "the moment" to occur. Surely, I'd get some revelation as to why God had forced me to catch a plane in the middle of a jam-packed week to head to some weird charismatic church in Kansas.

But nothing happened. I was beginning to feel a little ripped off, like God had used the craziest coincidence just to waste my time.

On the third day, after lunch, our small group of Hamilton pilgrims sat down with one of the pastors of Navah, who started telling his story. It wasn't particularly fantastic or interesting. But then something in it just . . . hit me. At a deep level. A soul level.

And I felt a little droplet pop out of the corner of my eye. And then a matching friend on the other side. And then . . . *oh crap.*

Full. On. Sob. Fest.

I was a heaving, drooling, snot-nosed disaster.

Our host finished his story and asked some people from their church to pray for us Hamiltonians. They prayed for inner healing, life direction, and all sorts of beautiful stuff. And then, after all that, he asked me a simple but brutal question: "Kevin, do you have any sin you need to repent of?" The gall of this guy. No. I'm fine. Self-sufficient. I'm not even crying; that was just a ploy to give you all a prayer exercise. But of course, in that moment, the Holy Spirit was actually present, challenging me, comforting me, and telling me this was the time.

"Matt . . ." I turned to my friend, "I have been so jealous of New Church."

Jesus looks Peter right in the eye and asks, "Do you love me?"
And Peter responds, "Yes, Lord, you know that I love you."

I carried on through spit and snot: "I've been jealous over how much everyone loves you guys and of how quickly you're growing and of how good your stupid musicians are . . . and I'm just really sad that people left our church."

And Jesus asks Peter a second time, "Peter, do you love me?"

And Peter responds a second time, "Yes, Lord, you know that I love you."

I caught my breath and pushed through the end of my confession: "I see how incredible your community is and how much good stuff you are experiencing, and it's just made me bitter. I'm sorry."

And finally, a third time, sitting next to a charcoal fire, Jesus asks, "Peter, do you love me?"

And Matt held my hands and said, "Kevin, I forgive you."

Poison and Its Antidote

Forgiveness may just be the most powerful force in the universe. And it's something the church has in her DNA. But we aren't used to it. Whenever someone confesses something to me, my default posture is to explain it away. "It's no big deal." "You tried your best." "Nobody is *perfect!*" But in this moment, Matt saw my envy for what it was: sin. A poison that, if left unchecked, would rot me away from the inside out. You can't shrug off poison and you can't explain it away. Only forgiveness can suck the toxin out of us.

Throughout this book, I've tried to share a number of reasons why the church is worth being a part of. This is one of those primordial elements of Christian community that is difficult and countercultural, but I can't overstate its significance: The church puts us in close enough proximity to other people that we *will* hurt each other. And then she gives us the only way to heal that wound.

The forgiveness that Christ spoke to Peter.

That God offers us.

Which Matt extended to me.

Which you can give to others.

And you can request from others.

Receiving forgiveness from Matt helped me to uncurl my own twisted heart, and once it was beating, my body functioned properly. I was able to see clearly again. Blake was growing in his new community, and I could take joy in it. I could celebrate that Sandra was still in relationship with people in our church and even showed up to some of our events. Their stories weren't done yet, but they didn't belong to me or even to Eucharist. They never did. God is writing their story and using the whole church to do so.

I had to get out of the way.

I returned to Hamilton with a new mission. Having been forgiven, I wanted to extend forgiveness to others. Just as hurt people hurt people, forgiven people forgive people.

That summer, I saw the couple who had gone through the accident and left our church. We were at a concert in the park, and the wife walked right up to us, said hello, and gave Meg and me an awkward hug. Then she introduced us to their newborn son and asked if I wanted to hold him.

I did.

I gently cradled his neck, looked down at his innocent face, and leaned forward to breathe him in.

And he smelled like charcoal fire.

11 CHURCH PLANT BOOT CAMP

Sixteen months after moving into First Christian Reformed Church, our fourth rental space, we packed up a moving truck, yet again, and drove down the street to another old church building around the corner from the one that had kicked us out. We should have been pros by this point, thrilled to finally be leaving purgatory, but instead, we moved more slowly and wore fewer smiles. This would be our fifth location in as many years. We had added quite a bit over the past year and a half: a dozen new pilgrims on the journey, a few buckets of kids' toys, and some new stories to share around the fire. But I felt like we had lost more than we had found. People who were core to our community had moved on, and their absence was palpable. Packing didn't feel like an adventure this time. It felt like a slog. You can only experience so many transitions before you start to wonder if you're just doing something wrong. Is our foundation crooked? Is God punishing us for some unconfessed sin? Are we cursed?

It didn't help that I was still feeling personal rejection from those who had left Eucharist. Some nights, I would lie awake in bed, tossing and turning as I played negative comments over and over in my mind. A few times, I shot straight up in the middle of the night, heart racing, worried that someone else core to the church might leave and take their friends with them, which would just result in more heartbreak, doubt, and grief for me and the community.

The worst was when I would get that ominous text: "Can we meet up?"

Fight-or-flight mode: activated. I immediately ran through the list of things I might have said or done that this person could be upset about. Did I say something they disagreed with? Did I miss their birthday? My thumbs frantically texted back, "What if I just jump off a bridge; will that fix things?" They usually just wanted brunch. But this low-level anxiety, this fear of rejection, was starting to really weigh on me. It was like a TV that only played static, constantly buzzing whether I was aware of it or not, and I wasn't sure how much more I could take.

I needed to escape.

The Baptists

I was on the edge of spiritually drowning when I got the phone call. It was Clark, who worked for the Baptists and who probably deserves an introduction at this point in the story. While Eucharist was a theological hybrid, made up of people from many different backgrounds, we had actually been associated with a particular denomination from day one: the oldest Baptist association in Canada. They didn't have a lot of money or infrastructure for starting new churches, but they were one of the few preexisting relationships I had when Eucharist was starting. A few of the churches in our TrueCity network were this brand of Baptist, and as I got to know them, I asked if the association would welcome our little sprout into the garden. They graciously made space for us but had been largely hands-off. Which made Clark's unexpected phone call all the more intriguing.

He asked if Meg and I would be willing to go to an assessment process run by one of the country's largest church planting organizations. The truth is that very few church communities start like we did. They often begin more like a tech start-up, with retreats and three-day incubators, after which the church planter is given a pass or fail. The difference is that, in the Christian world, the question isn't whether investors will give money or not. This incubator has a higher aim: at the end of the discernment process, the assessors will tell you whether God himself has called you to do this work or if you've been wrong in your desire to start a church.

Of course, the timing for this was . . . unconventional. If we weren't called by God to church plant, then what exactly were we up to all these years?

Clark shared that, of course, he had no doubt we were called to church plant but that the denomination was interested in seeing more churches start and hoped this organization would be a good resource. They wanted us to be the guinea pigs, to run through the process and share our experience. "At the same time," he tagged on, "I personally think it's a great chance for you to understand more about your gifts. These people are professionals, they've done this assessment for hundreds of successful church planters, and whatever their conclusion is will be helpful for you guys." It was subtle and may have been more in my head than in his words, but as the conversation progressed, I felt there was another unspoken agenda: "We also want to know if you are *really* supposed to be doing this."

Lastly, he pointed out that this particular organization, when they affirm a church planter, rains down upon the church tens of thousands of dollars, filling a baptismal tank with gold, Scrooge McDuck–style. The devil on my shoulder whispered, *Think about all the napping the church could do with an extra $50,000.*

Then I graciously declined the offer.

I was already exhausted and dealing with heightened sensitivity. The idea of being thrown into the lion's den wasn't exactly the beachside escape I was looking for. But Clark sweetened the deal: the assessment was in Vancouver, and the denomination would pay for Meg and me to head out a week early and come back a week late. We could have a proper two-week vacation, with an itty-bitty church plant assessment for a few days in between.

So that's how we ended up flying across the country, hoping to find out if we were meant to do the thing we'd already been doing for five years.

Shadowy Figures

We spent the first week in Vancouver meeting with friends and drinking an obscene amount of coffee. We rented a car and drove through the mountains. The winding paths offered a generous view of the ocean below, while snow-covered peaks loomed on the horizon. The space itself ministered to us. We took deep breaths, and the West Coast air filled our lungs. "You are the beloved of God," a seagull squawked as it tried to eat our french fries, "and nothing you do or don't do will change that!"

After several days of rest, we packed up our luggage and took a train into the suburbs to the large megachurch that would host our assessment. We walked in and met the other nine people who were going through the process. "Hello, everyone. Thanks for coming!" said our greeter. "These are the worksheets for the next few days," she said, handing out binders stuffed to overflowing. "And this is the itinerary for our time together."

Meg and I pulled out the schedule and tried to decipher it. Colored blocks of time ran into and over other colored blocks of time. Twelve-hour days, packed to the brim with meetings, activities, and interviews. We'd be dismissed at 8:30 p.m. and were expected back at the building at 8:00 a.m. Also, there was homework every night.

We walked into a classroom and were asked to choose a seat at one of three tables, arranged in a semicircle, facing the whiteboard. Then the assessors walked in and sat in the large semicircle behind us, a literal board of shadowy figures who observed our every move and typed away whenever we spoke, coughed, or breathed. Then the lead assessor marched in, arms swinging through the air, head held high, like he was assessing for WrestleMania. He introduced us to his team.

There were twenty-five of them in total: one woman running logistics, one woman running exercises with her husband, and twenty-three white, middle-aged men.

Now, I don't have an issue with middle-aged white guys per se; I'm already two-thirds of the way there. But I did wonder how they could assess anything when they had such a narrow perspective of the human experience, never mind the Imago Dei, which is revealed in every person and culture. How could they help plant churches that would connect with the whole range of humanity when they filtered everyone through such an exclusive lens? Meg and I slowly took our seats, trying to communicate how we were feeling using only eye contact. We were trying our best to be sober-minded and grounded, but I was already beginning to sweat profusely. Meg must have seen my glistening forehead. She leaned over to me and touched my hand. "Okay, so this isn't going to be the most natural fit for us," she whispered to me, "but there's still lots we can learn here." We had decided in advance that we would not accept any money offered to us, no matter the perceived lack of strings attached. We knew the only way to walk through this assessment honestly would be to remove the temptation of that sweet cash money. We even told the leadership team from Eucharist so that we couldn't back out if they snuck up on us with one of those giant, reality-show checks. "Since we don't need the money," Meg said, "let's just be honest. We don't want to play *the game*."

You know the game, right? The one so often played in Christian circles. You say what the leadership wants to hear, stick to the theological party lines, and quote quirky Christian mantras like "Love the sinner, hate the sin" and "Let's love on them for Jesus" (you know, the sort of weird stuff that anyone who isn't a part of Christian subculture is confused and a little creeped out by). You smile widely, fake laugh out loud when no one said anything funny, quote a lot of Scripture with some John Calvin sprinkled on top, and whatever you do—no matter what tragedies or horrors befall you—don't swear.

Seriously. Four-letter words are a guaranteed way to lose the "Christian game."

I went to seminary. I knew how to play the game. But if "Fake Kevin" and "Fake Meg" ran through the assessment, we'd only be able to hear what God was saying to our fake selves. Sure, we weren't a perfect fit for this assessment process, but that also excited me. It's one thing to be affirmed by our mentors and friends, but if a bunch of strangers who didn't know us saw God working in Eucharist, then we could finally be certain that this was important.

Everything had led to this weekend.

Meadow Creek

Now that the room was filled, we all went around the circle and introduced ourselves, our city and context, and why we wanted to church plant someday (or in our case, why we had already church planted years ago and how it was a little weird to go through this discernment for a thing we had already done). Couple after couple went up and shared until it got to the only unmarried person in the room. Immediately, the leader of the assessment joked about him being single: "Don't worry, we'll fix that soon!" he assured him with a wink.

Groan.

It just got weirder from there. Fingers danced over the keyboards, frantic clicks whenever we answered a question. We were placed in groups to do exercises that tested our leadership skills and ability to work together. We were blindfolded and led around a room to solve word problems and logic puzzles. It felt like the Riddler had given up on trying to defeat Batman and was now hell-bent on finding the best church planters in the country. These activities were broken up by lunches, during which assessors would casually sit down with us "to hang," but these faux interviews were as obvious as Bugs Bunny in drag. "So, Kevin, just asking for no real reason at all," the assessor said with a casual twirl of spaghetti, "how do you confront the sin in your neighbors' lives without compromising on gospel integrity, while continuing to abide in a missiological framework of trust, vis-à-vis eschatological urgency?" Through the whole meal, I'd be doing mental gymnastics in my head: *What are they really trying to ask? How much do I say? Should I just tell them what they want to hear?*

At one point, we were told to create a mock church plant and pitch it to the assessors. We tried the best we could, but it was difficult to feel invested in a fictional congregation designed for a neighborhood none of us had ever visited before. But during this activity, there was a shift in the room. After three days of awkward, half-hearted connection, we loosened up and became honest with one another. We all admitted we had no idea what a hypothetical church should look like, but we had a growing sense of what it shouldn't be. "It shouldn't be so cookie-cutter," one person observed. "It's easy for churches to feel like they were built in a lab or by a committee." Another affirmed, "Totally. It should reflect the people and place it's planted in, not just emulate some other big church."

We hit a wall when trying to name our congregation (because healthy plants need a killer brand), and started riffing on generic church names:

"Let's call it Meadow Creek!"
"No, Creek Side!"
"Hill Crest?"
"Mountain Valley?"
"North Tree?"
"Tree of Hope."
"Hope Hill."

"Calvary Hill."

"Calvary Side."

"Christ's Side on Calvary Peak!"

"Jesus's Church."

"Christ Church . . . of Holy Spirit!"

"Christ Church of Holy Spirit, of Prophecy . . . of FIRE!"

We were laughing so loudly, and for the first time, the group felt inspired. We needed to be honest, to spend some time naming all the ways the church has missed the mark, so that we could begin to reclaim her for all she's meant to be.

Just then, the door flew open, and one of the assessors stormed into the room. "*You guys are not taking this seriously!*" he yelled at us, his finger wagging in our faces. "The real world is full of people who are *going to hell* and you're in here *laughing it up*!" He marched out of the room and slammed the door behind him. We stared at each other, mouths wide open. It felt like the principal had just broken a ruler on the chalkboard. The joy in the room had been entirely depleted, and we got back to the boring, soul-sucking work of dreaming up the future of the church. To his credit, the man who yelled at us later apologized for his outburst, and we forgave him and tried to move on, but it revealed something troubling at a deeper level. There was a lot of fear and anxiety brewing just below the surface. It felt so unlike the nonanxious, nonaggressive, deeply rooted people who had kept our church sane over the past few years.

In addition to the assessors, two psychologists were brought in for the weekend. They also seemed uncomfortable with the way things were going. In one of our meetings with them, Meg asked a question that hit the nail on the head: "Why is everyone here so angry?"

It didn't feel like we were planting churches out of love but out of fear.

The whole thing was exhausting. And of course, that was the point. This wasn't a discernment process; it was a boot camp. It was "Church Plant *Hunger Games*," designed to see what we're made of. And while that may sound like a quick way to get the best churches started, I'm not convinced it's the way God actually works. For Eucharist, church planting was hard work but also a great adventure. There were seasons of suffering, but the whole thing was steeped in such a deep joy. It was born out of an overflow of love for Hamilton and the people who lived there. When we were first dreaming up the church in our living room, friends had warned us that church planting would be hard, and it was. But it was also so much fun.

I suspect if the assessment hadn't been shaped by so many white middle-aged men, we would have seen a very different type of discernment process.

Back in our hotel room, before getting to our homework, Meg and I ate junk food and sprawled out on the stiff hotel mattress. We talked about the board of shadowy figures behind us and how we all got yelled at, and then I wrote down as much as we could recall. The whole thing was so surreal that we had to remember the details forever. People back home must have felt their spiritual spider sense tingling.

On the second day, I got a text from Bishop Dave: "Don't drink the Kool-Aid."

Evangelize Me

One of the strangest moments of the assessment process was when Meg and I were called into a room to do an evangelism exercise. We sat across from two of the men who explained that seeing people "get saved" is a big part of church planting, and they wanted to see if we had the gift of evangelism necessary to start the church (that we had already started). "I'm going to be someone who doesn't know Jesus, and I want you to evangelize me," the man on the left said, as if this was a perfectly normal thing to do. "So tell me about someone you know who isn't a Christian."

"Alright," I said, flipping through my mental Rolodex of "unsaved" neighbors. "There's my friend Lily. She is a brilliant, bighearted, single mother who I met at a coffee shop downtown." Just thinking about Lily, her hospitality, her bear hugs, and her oyster-shucking parties, made me smile. "She wasn't raised in a Christian environment but in a moderately secular Jewish household. Over the last few months, she has started to hang out with some people from the church and has even attended some gatherings."

"Perfect," he replied enthusiastically. "I'll be Lily, and you evangelize me," which is a weird thing to say, and it made me a little uncomfortable to see my friend becoming a prop in a boot-camp game on the other side of the country. But I *was* trying to be open.

I collected my thoughts, took a breath, and said to the middle-aged man across the table from me, "Okay . . . Lily . . . you were raised in a Jewish household, but you said it was quite secular. Can you tell me more about what that was like for you?" Silence. Blank stares back from "Lily," who I am now realizing didn't sign up for an improv activity.

"No, no, I think you missed the point of this exercise," he said with a dismissive hand wave. "I want you to evangelize to me."

"That's what I'm doing . . ." I responded.

"No, no," he replied, confused, "I mean I want you to lead me to Christ."

"Well, I figure we've got to start somewhere," I said back. "I don't know anything about you, your story, where you come from, or how you see the world. I'm curious what religion looks like to you and how you've seen God in your life so far."

"Okay, fine, fine," he said, rubbing his forehead, "but let's move past all that. Let's imagine I've been around for a few months already and you know my story and background. Convert me!"

With a chipper, "Okay, let's do it," I launched into evangelism mode. "So, Lily, you've been around the church community for a few months now; can you tell me what has stuck out to you?" "She" looked back, visibly frustrated, and with a clearly annoyed voice replied, "Kevin, we're well beyond that point . . ." Suddenly, the other assessor in the room interrupted and banged his hand on the table. He leaned in and spoke through gritted teeth, "Why are you being difficult? You know what we are looking for: She's lying on her deathbed. *Close the deal!*"

Now I was pissed. My friend Lily was someone I loved, who was made in the image of God and not going to be used as a prop in some religious sales tactic. "Close the deal?" I snapped back. "We're talking about God and trust and hope and eternity . . . I'm not selling her a freaking car!" Except, I didn't say freaking. No, no, no. I was so frustrated with the way evangelism was being removed from relationship, how the mystery of God's grace was being mechanized, that in a moment of blind passion, I said the big one. The four-letter one.

The one you aren't *ever* supposed to say in polite Christian company.

You know what is really ironic? I actually love talking about God with people who aren't Christian. Wanting to share the Good News was the reason we started a church in the first place. But it had only ever been fruitful within relationships, a normal activity of discovering what the Holy Spirit was up to, which had resulted in many people coming to trust Jesus with their lives. The evangelism exercise should have been where I shone.

If they had wanted me to fail, they should have given me an email exercise.

Five Ways This Can Go

The assessors had been up all night, debating in a conference room with whiteboards and reports, fueled by prayer and Red Bull. After three twelve-hour days of grueling psychological and spiritual warfare, it was the moment of truth. We all sat in a hallway together and waited as each couple was called into the small office where they would receive word from on high: the official assessment.

Finally, it was our turn.

"Now, there are five ways this can go," the lead assessor said to us, laying out the options:

"If we give you an A, that's a 'Full Pass': God is calling you to church plant, and we will support you fully in that calling.

"B is a 'Light Pass': God is calling you to church plant, but we have some light reservations about your theology or character, and we want to help you get right in those areas. We'll connect you with a mentor for a few years of coaching before you plant.

"C is 'Serious Reservations': We have some real concerns about your theology or character, but God *may* be calling you to church plant. We want to help you continue to grow and discern over the next few years before doing this assessment again.

"D is a 'Helper Pass': We think you should be involved in a church plant, but not as the senior pastor. We see that God is doing something in your life around church plants and new expressions, but you should not be the lead planter."

Reaching the end of the list, the bottom of the barrel, he concluded: "Finally, an F is a 'No Pass': God has not called you to church plant, and to do so would put your community and your own soul in jeopardy."

There was a brief silence, and I could almost hear my heart racing. "Your case was a little unconventional, as you two have already planted a church," the assessor said, flipping through the papers before him. "But we decided to ignore that fact and treat you just like everybody else."

Three days of madness had led to this. The official word from the largest and most successful church planting movement in the country was:

"Kevin, after much prayer and discernment, our assessment is F. God has not called you to church plant."

12 EVERYTHING WE'RE NOT

"Kevin, after much prayer and discernment, our assessment is F. God has not called you to church plant."

For the record, this is really awkward news to bring home to your church plant.

Even after saying a certain four-letter word, I thought we were still in "C: 'Serious Reservations'" territory. That would make sense. Most days, I have serious reservations about myself. But to hear, in no uncertain terms, that *God* had declared that Eucharist shouldn't exist was a little intense.

"Kevin, there are two reasons you failed," the assessor said to me, looking at the paper before him. "Number one: You have a low social aptitude," to which I wanted to respond, "Listen, buddy. There are a lot of things I am bad at, but the whole 'people thing' isn't one of them."

The second reason hurt a little more. "We don't believe you're a strong enough Christian to do this," the assessor said, looking over his notes. "If something good is happening in the congregation you have already planted, it is a product of your own personal strengths and not the Lord working through your weaknesses."

This is one of those Christian statements that drive me crazy. I know full well that God works through our weaknesses, but of course, he also uses our strengths. In their minds, if things were going well, it was our own strengths at work, but if things were going poorly, then it was clear God wasn't blessing us.

Through that lens, it was impossible to see God at work in Eucharist.

After the formal reasons, the other assessor jumped in with a few off-the-cuff observations: "It's also because you couldn't close the deal with the evangelism exercise." They told us that church plants needed to have clearer lines around who is in and who is out, that we can't just point people to Jesus, but we also need to tell them what to believe and how to act. Despite all the struggles we had experienced, I really believed we were discovering something beautiful about the church. Clearly we were wrong. The experts had spoken.

Meg and I left the room in a daze and carpooled back to the hotel with another couple from the boot camp. They got a B: "Light Pass." We talked and prayed together in the parking lot, and they encouraged us to just take the good and leave the bad. But it wasn't so easy.

We hadn't been given a hunch or an educated guess. This was a crystal clear "word from God."

Dallas

The morning after getting an F, Meg and I took the train to Seattle. We didn't talk much. When we weren't napping to recover our energy, we stared out the window and watched the coast scroll past. When the train eventually stopped, we made our way to our rental house and ordered enough tacos to fill the sad, empty hole in our hearts. That evening, my phone rang. It was Dallas, a friend from Hamilton who copastored another Baptist church with his wife, Leanne.

Dallas spent years meeting with me as Eucharist found her footing. We had originally connected through the TrueCity network of churches, but he quickly became a spiritual big brother. When our charitable status hit a speed bump, his church legally adopted us for two years. When Eucharist was going well, we ate chicken wings and celebrated. When it felt like everything was falling apart, I'd lie on the floor of his sanctuary and yell hypothetical questions at him. His style of pastoral care was stealthy. He never told me what to do and rarely offered his own opinions. Instead, he'd ask a perfectly placed question that, as I responded, would blow the doors of my soul wide open. That made plenty of space for the Holy Spirit to work. Few people knew the heart of our congregation like Dallas, which is why, when the boot camp requested information about us in advance of the assessment, he spent hours filling out form after form about Eucharist. By the time he got to the question, written in King James language, "Does the applicant properly divide the Word of Truth?" he was worried the assessors might not "get" us. But when he heard their conclusion, he felt blindsided.

"What if they're right, Dallas?" I asked him as Meg and I huddled around the phone, which was on speaker mode. "What if we aren't meant to be a church? What if it's just our natural gifts that have gotten us here?" There was a moment of silence, and I waited for one of those well-placed Dallas questions, but instead, he laughed and said, "Do you actually think you guys are that gifted?" Meg and I stared at each other, a little offended, but he continued. "Remember when you came to that first TrueCity meeting in the coffee shop, how you were twenty-three and had no idea what you were doing? Remember how you guys moved five times in the first five years? Have you forgotten how many established churches and wiser saints had to come alongside Eucharist so that she wouldn't fall on her face?" This was not the encouraging pep talk we had been anticipating. "Kevin, by every human metric, this church plant should have imploded within the first six months, but instead, she's flourished because God is totally at work in Eucharist." He paused to let the words sink in before finishing his argument. "Why would you forget all of that just because a few guys in the suburbs of Vancouver didn't understand what God was doing in downtown Hamilton?"

He was right. There is a time for discernment, for asking hard questions about what to do with our energy, our time, or our money. Sometimes that discernment means getting a professional opinion or even attending a boot camp. But we were years into Eucharist and had seen too much good fruit to believe we were a bad tree. God was in this.

The assessors were just flat-out wrong.

Once I recognized that they were incorrect, I was also able to see that they were half right: we weren't supposed to be a church *like they imagined church should be.*

The Body

In the second year of Eucharist, I preached through the New Testament letter called 1 Corinthians. It was written by the apostle Paul, who lived in the city of Corinth for over a year and a half, trying to cultivate a new Christian community. He eventually left and entrusted the congregation to good teachers, including one named Apollos. He was confident that God was at work. But when he finally got an update on his beloved community, he learned that it had become a tire fire.

Christians in the Corinthian church were suing one another because they couldn't work out their conflicts within the family. People were debating who their favorite Bible teacher was, with some wearing "Team Apollos" T-shirts and others cheering for #teamPaul. Even their potlucks, the best sign of the kingdom of God we've got, had become a total mess. The rich, who naturally brought more food and better wine, decided they didn't want to share with those who were poor. Instead, the wealthy started gathering early to eat all the good food and drink all of the wine. Only after they were bloated and hammered did they allow the poor to come eat the scraps. When Paul heard about this, he was angry and grieved. They had completely failed to live out the radical unity of the Good News. So he wrote them a letter and gave them a powerful image of what the church is:

The human body is made up of many different parts, but each part works for the good of the whole. In some ways, Paul says, our bodies appear to be disjointed. Imagine you're an alien visiting earth for the first time and you walk into a room and see a hand, an eyeball, a toenail, and a lung sitting on the table. I imagine you'd have some questions, chief among them: "Whose house is this?" But you might also wonder what these four objects are, and how they are connected. They look radically different from one another. If you were told they were all part of the same body, you might even push back: one is fleshy, one is squishy and covered in blood, and one of them appears to be a small bell. How can they be one? But, of course, every part is connected to the whole, and each has a role to play.

This, Paul says, is what the body of Christ is like. In every community, there are different people with different backgrounds and gifts who, together, become the body of Christ. It only functions because each part brings something unique to the whole. Our ears let us hear, our tongue grants us taste and speech, and our toes give us balance. The wider church is also meant to function as a body.

It is all congregations across the globe, through time and space, in different expressions and languages, cultures and backgrounds, that together become the true body of Christ.

It's as if the assessment gurus were used to examining hands. They had looked at hundreds of hands and could predict which ones were strong enough to handle being scraped and cut, which ones could warmly greet visitors and straighten out crooked paths.

But then a foot walked into the assessment center, and they were confused. "Why are its fingers so short?" they asked with suspicion. "And why does it have a heel on its palm?" When the time came to fill out a report, they told the foot it was, in fact, not a part of the body because it didn't look like a hand at all. But the foot was strong enough to walk with those who were far away from home and nimble enough to traverse uncertain territory. The foot could handle the dirt and grime of downtown Hamilton, going places a hand never could.

I don't think other congregations should necessarily do what we've done. We took audacious risks that could have sunk a larger ship, played fast and loose with holy days in a way that would make my childhood pastor nervous, and made weird art projects featuring saints with blood on their hands and gigantic Christmas monsters. We still host annual funerals for Jesus and Nap Sundays. And we're uncomfortably honest and noncontrolling. Every Sunday, congregants are welcome to write out prayers, which are then read verbatim in front of the community. This has resulted in the whole congregation praying everything from "Go Raptors" to "Please make my crush like me back."

I get it, Eucharist is freaking weird. Not every church should be a foot like us. I'll go one step further: most churches shouldn't be like us.

But we should be us.

There are many parts in the body of Christ. Some are a pinky; others are an eyelash or that little thing that hangs at the back of your throat. Some parts are large and easy on the eyes; others are small and less pretty. But for the body to be whole, each part is indispensable.

Rejection

The following week in Seattle was enjoyable for Meg and me, but a dark cloud still followed us everywhere. When we went back to our place at night, I had to fight the temptation to revisit the reports given to us by the boot camp. Talking to Dallas had convinced me the assessors were wrong, but slowly my sadness was morphing into what I perceived as righteous anger. I wanted to post their content on social media and begin a crusade against church organizations who couldn't see that the body of Christ was bigger than their particular expression.

But if I did that, was I really acting any different?

In that same section of 1 Corinthians, the apostle Paul wrote, "The eye cannot say to the hand, 'I have no need of you,' nor again the head to the feet, 'I have no need of you.'"

It hurt to be judged wrongly, but we had a chance to forgive, to recognize that, despite the pain, we were still in this body together. The assessors, like us, wanted to follow Jesus in a complicated world. They were trying to steward their resources to see God's kingdom come. They were trusting in the same grace we were.

For better or for worse, we're all one in the body.

That body includes Sandra and Bishop Dave, Jake, Eric, and Dopey Eyes. It's made up of everyone who walked away from Eucharist and everyone who has stuck around. It's big enough for St. Barnabas, who kicked us out; the Reformed congregation, who hosted us for a year; and New Church, who I am now only *slightly* jealous of. The body is made up of FT, where I broke bread under my armpit, of the Lutheran Church (Missouri Synod), as well as the "other" Lutheran Church. And I thank God for this gracious, grand body because it has room for me, a pastor who is still learning, growing, and fumbling forward.

So yes, of course, the body of Christ includes the assessors who flunked us.

You

In light of all that, how do we know what part of the body we're called to be a part of?

Some reading this are already connected to a church community, and while I don't know exactly what she looks like, I know she matters deeply. While I clearly have a soft spot for small, unimpressive congregations, perhaps your church is large and flashy, made up of thousands of people making a massive impact. That is amazing. Don't shy away from the size or scale of your work, but perhaps you can be one of the people who appreciate your community for the less obvious reasons. Rather than celebrating results, learn to give thanks for the many people sacrificing their time, energy, and money to see the church become all she is meant to be. Jesus may *appreciate* that she is impactful and important, but that's *not why* he loves her.

Perhaps, on the other end of the spectrum, the church you belong to is so tiny no one has ever heard of her. Maybe you feel that if she only had more people, more money, or a little more influence, she could really make an impact. But there are positives to being smaller: you can be intensely attentive to one another, you can all pray together in one room, or you can easily gather together outside of Sunday. There are things you can do with fifteen people that you can't do with fifteen thousand.

Perhaps you are someone who has walked away from the church or never quite had the courage to walk through the front door. Maybe you've seen plenty worth critiquing in the congregations around you. But the older I get, the more I've come to believe that it's in our limitation and weakness that we truly experience grace and love. I'm not saying you should go find a church that functions like an abusive spouse, but I am encouraging you to find an imperfect church, one as beat-up and flawed as you are. Start as small and near as possible, and take the time to discover what's beautiful there.

Some of you may not be ready to step into a church building or community, and that's okay also. Sometimes the pain associated with church is so intense that even being in religious spaces or hearing "churchy" language can be so triggering that it's almost impossible to connect with God. Receive this as your blessing to step away, at least for a season, and see where else the Spirit will meet you. I pray that in time, as God brings reconciliation and healing, you'll know what to do next.

Maybe you have been engaged in a local church for months or years, but it has become clear over time this is not the part of the body you are called to be with. Throughout this book, I've spoken often about church unity and the power of it, but there are times when, for the good of the whole body, you need to join another community. But if you decide to leave your congregation and connect with a different expression, please do it well. Talk to the people you need to talk to. Be humble and gracious as you go. Try to leave with a blessing, knowing that you aren't joining a "different church" at all but simply putting your energy into another part of the same body.

Finally, some of you reading this feel like I did at twenty-three years old, with a fire in your belly to see a new kind of church community emerge. If the horror stories of this book haven't dissuaded you, perhaps you're cut out for the work. But you may not have to start a whole new congregation in order to do something new in the church. You can form a group of peers who worship together midweek, and then find an older church that can adopt you on Sunday. You could start a morning prayer time or a monthly worship evening while still being connected to a more established congregation. There are so many creative ways to see new things grow. With all that said, if you are truly inspired to start a new church community, one that can connect with people and places the traditional church hasn't, know that I'm with you. Some parts of the body of Christ have become atrophied, and maybe a few of you are called to wake them up.

Find some friends, break some bread, root yourself in a place, and pay attention to what God is growing.

Return

Kanye West has this great line on his *Graduation* album: "Everything I'm not made me everything I am." I find that lyric really insightful. We can spend a long time trying to be some other person, some other church, all the while missing the unique part of the body we are called to be. The bad news is that sometimes we have to be rejected or experience failure to recognize what we aren't. The good news is, failure and rejection are great teachers.

After a restful week in Seattle, we landed back in Hamilton. Ontario's winter air was still cold and dry, but our hearts were warmed by driving through the city we loved. We met up with Dallas and Leanne a few days later to debrief in person. Before we even started talking, they handed us a sealed envelope. "Open it!" they said, leaning forward like excited puppies with their tails wagging.

Inside was a beautiful, elaborate certificate:

"This Document Certifies that Kevin Makins and Meg Makins Are Hereby Recommended for Church Planting by Friesen & Friesen Church Plant Assessment Center by Rev. Leanne Friesen and Rev. Dallas Friesen."

On the back was a list of qualifications, each with a checkbox next to it:

Hearts for Justice: Check.

Being Awesome: Check.

Great Bangs: Check.

Love for God and Neighbor: Check.

Have Actually Planted an Amazing Church: Check.

The next Sunday, Meg and I stood in front of Eucharist and had to tell them the bad news that we weren't supposed to exist. We walked through the whole story and, at the end, told them what I've just told you. That we were a valuable part of the big, expansive body of Christ and that we'd continue to love who God made us to be.

The congregation gave us a standing ovation.

It wasn't us thinking we were better than any other church or above having others speak into our lives. It was a recognition that we weren't a hand or an eye or an ear. We were a different part of the body.

Everything we're not made us everything we are.

13 DYING WELL

The early church started with a bang. The Holy Spirit exploded onto the scene, sparking a wildfire that spread overnight. The followers of Jesus sold all their possessions and gave the money to the poor. Some were arrested and put on trial. Every day was an adventure, and the church grew larger and larger. But then there was controversy: those who distributed the food were giving more to church members who shared their ethnic background and overlooking those who did not.

So the disciples pulled together a team who would ensure everyone was being treated fairly, which must have meant taking inventory of what they had and arranging proper channels of communication.

The second chapter of Acts describes the coming of the Holy Spirit and the birth of the church. By chapter 6, they're arranging tables and using spreadsheets.

The church is only four chapters old and she's already striking committees.

What is so fascinating to me is that it was no longer enough for the early church to move ahead. They had to maintain what they had. As annoying as it is, perhaps this organizational stuff is also part of being the church. It's one thing to pioneer into the wilderness but quite another to create a home in the wild.

New Pastor

Failing boot camp had clarified to me how important Eucharist was, but there was still the question of how we would continue to grow. In our sixth year, we hired a church consultant to help us figure out next steps, and after a few meetings, he told us what the problem was. "The problem is Kevin," he said to the room. "He is never going to be organized enough to make this church sustainable."

We all knew he was right. Some churches need help getting outside of their walls or becoming "missional"—we needed spreadsheets and filing cabinets. The leadership team asked me to leave the room while they discussed some options, and when they invited me back in, they told me I should rearrange the office. We were going to have two pastors.

Thankfully I never arranged the office in the first place.

A few months later, I was sitting across from Jill Trites, who had spent twenty years working in the business world before going to seminary to become a counselor. Jill had spent the past few years running a support group for women who had been victims of sex trafficking, and on the side, she served on the leadership team for the TrueCity network. When Bishop Dave heard about the job posting that would soon go live, he set us up on a blind date.

We held down a small table with a steady supply of caffeine. After walking through her career so far, Jill was closing out her story. "So that's where I'm at, completely unsure of what to do next. I've spent half of my life in the business and leadership world," she said, raising one hand, "and half of my life in the church and counseling world," she continued, raising the other. "I'm just trying to figure out how to connect the two." Her hands came together, fingers intertwined. "To be honest, Kevin, I have no freaking idea what is next, so I've told God I'm just going to continue saying yes to whatever he drops before me." She laughed and took a sip of coffee. "So there's my story . . . what did you want to talk about?"

Jill ended up going through the whole job application process with us, which was far more intense than we had any right to make it. Three interviews, three reference checks, two congregational check-ins, and one haiku later (yes, we requested poetry), we were formally introducing our second pastor to the congregation. Eucharist was always an engaged community, but everyone else had other stuff going on, so the buck always stopped with me. Now, for the first time, I wasn't alone.

There was someone else giving their full-time energy to nurturing this community, and she was so much better at email than me.

With Jill on staff, our congregation found a sense of stability we had never had before. Our partnership created a healthy tension for the church. We continued to experiment with new projects, but we also wrote up policies and procedures. We launched an artist coworking space, but also made a master calendar. Everyone picked up on the changes. Young families felt we were organized enough to keep their kids safe, older congregants no longer felt like they were babysitting a youth group, and even the artists appreciated getting reimbursed for their supplies. Together we were able to integrate and spur on the different sides of the congregation.

We gave Jill the official job title, "Pastor of Systems and Structures," which allowed me to adopt my revised job title, "Pastor of Blowing Things Up."

"I Run a Bar"

When Eucharist started, I assumed we'd never have a building. Church buildings have leaks and mice and dust and furnaces to repair and sidewalks to shovel. I could barely remember to charge my phone every day. And besides, all those old buildings were practically museums, relics of a time long past, when Christianity was powerful and culturally influential. Around us, we saw so many church communities who were stuck with burdensome buildings tied like millstones around their necks. We were free of all those pressures, able to rent any space we wanted for a fraction of what it would cost to own one.

Why would we ever put on that old yoke of slavery?

Shortly after hiring Jill, I ran into a friend at a party. He's a Hamilton staple who, when he isn't playing live music at famous festivals around the world, runs a small bar on our street. He started telling me about his new dream. "I'm looking around at all these old churches that have thirty people in them once a week, and I'm realizing they'd make perfect music venues. So I've been cold-calling them. Last week, I'm talking to this church right downtown, and they've shrunk to a dozen people. The building looks like crap from the outside, but I'm thinking maybe it's a good deal. We're talking, and they're open to selling it, but then—" he leaned in closer, "—they ask me what church I go to. And I tell them I don't go to church . . . I run a bar. And then they weren't interested in talking anymore." He chuckled. Then he added, "But, Makins, you guys are a church. You should call them."

I had no interest in buying a building. But why not make a phone call?

A few weeks later, our leadership team was sitting in the sanctuary of the Romanian Baptist Church. Forty years ago, when they had young families and boundless energy, they had purchased the building off of Victoria Baptist Church, which in the 1970s was itself an aging congregation. As their children grew up, they either stopped going to church or attended English-speaking congregations. Now the congregation was getting older, shrinking in size, and no longer able to ward off the leaking water and neighborhood rats trying to infiltrate the 125-year-old sanctuary. As they told us the story, I let my eyes wander around the room. Cracks ran up the walls to open gaps in the plaster. The old vinyl flooring was falling apart, beaten down with small circular imprints, the result of thousands of women in high heels walking through the space for over a hundred years.

Then I saw movement out of the corner of my eye and focused my vision to see more clearly. I apologetically cut into the conversation. "Excuse me, I don't mean to interrupt," I said to one of the Romanian Baptists, "but is that . . . is that a squirrel?" Yes. It was a squirrel. Just hanging out on top of a pew in the sanctuary.

"Oh, that happens sometimes," one of them said as he shuffled off to the back row to scare the critter out.

As I looked around the beautiful but decrepit sanctuary and watched everyone chase a squirrel around the room, I thought to myself, *Why would we want to take this on?* A few months later, the Romanian Baptists phoned Jill: "We can't stop thinking about the conversation we had with you all. We think God wants us to sell you the building."

Back in the Factory

This new opportunity raised all sorts of pressing questions: Are we a church called to steward a building or live a nomadic life? Can we afford to purchase, renovate, and carry the costs of an old building? How would we shape a space, and how would it shape us?

The Romanian Baptists needed an answer within the month, which left us only a few weeks to make a decision. We started by inviting the congregation to come see the building. Nearly a hundred of us walked through the space one evening and felt a mix of excitement and dread. The leadership team had asked me to do a short presentation on what could happen if we decided to buy a building, and as I worked on my talk, my fears and hesitations started to melt away. I began to imagine all the amazing stuff that could happen in this historic space if we were willing to take a risk. After renting five different buildings, we were well aware of the downsides of not having our own permanent space. I knew buying a building would be challenging—it might even kill us—but it would be worth it to throw ourselves into an adventure once again.

What can I say? I'm an Acts 2–5 kind of guy.

The community walked through the sanctuary and eventually gathered in the front pews, chatting with one another and bouncing babies on laps. I hushed the room and put a slideshow up on the wall. The first image was an imposing diagram of all the projects we had worked on and ministries we had partnered with over the history of our church. I walked us through our whole story so far, finally arriving at this opportunity. I talked about the radical decline of Christianity in Canada, how these religious buildings were being sold to condo developers, and how they would never return to the church again. Bouncing around the stage, I talked about statistics and geography and laid out a dozen ways we could use this building to reclaim church for good.

"What if . . ." I exclaimed dramatically, "what if this building wasn't something we hoarded for ourselves, but something we stewarded for the community?" I even made a little logo for the nonexistent organization: "The Center for Faith, Justice, and the Arts."

And as I painted a picture of the next decade, I felt like we were back in the small factory room on Launch Sunday, once again dreaming of the future, on the edge of the boat and ready to walk into our storm. When I finished the presentation, I looked out at the faces in the room, expecting to see them leaning forward, excited to dive back in.

Instead, I saw open jaws and sunken eyes.

Everyone was completely overwhelmed.

It wasn't day one of our church plant, and we weren't in the factory.

We had grown up.

We weren't dreaming about a new community. We were making a decision as an incarnated, flesh-and-blood church.

That's when I realized that we were about to make the most significant decision yet . . . and I wouldn't be the only one driving the vision this time. Whatever we decided would have to be done as a community. We were going to have to listen to the Holy Spirit together.

Talk + Pray

We gathered the community in smaller groups for "Talk + Pray" evenings, where we would simply sit in a circle, pray for an hour, and then talk for sixty more minutes. There were a number of "table manners" we asked people to follow so that people didn't get in fistfights. The hardest rule for me to follow was the "Kevin, just shut up and trust the community" rule. The leadership team put me on mute for the meetings.

The good news was that, when I stopped responding to every question, it created a space for other people to share. "I don't know if Eucharist is mature enough to handle this responsibility," someone said. There was a moment of silence and then another person responded, "You know, I have been a part of this community since day one, and a few years ago, I would have agreed with you. But I think that we've really grown up, and we might be able to handle this."

"I think this is a great use of our resources," said a young man in our community, adding, "We won't get another opportunity like this."

"That's true," the woman across the circle responded, "but maybe that should tell us that the days of owning buildings are gone, and we'd be better off investing in other projects."

People shared comments and insights: some rambling and passionate, others careful and articulate.

Over the next month, we held a number of Talk + Pray evenings, and things began to get clearer. The questions shifted. No longer were people asking what was right or wrong. Instead, they were fundamentally concerned with keeping unity no matter what decision we made. During the last Talk + Pray evening, Bishop Dave shared his thoughts. "I am beginning to think," he said softly, leaning forward in his seat, "that this isn't so much about whether Eucharist needs a building as it is about this building needing a church. God may be calling us to breathe new life into this space for the next 125 years."

At the end of the month, we invited those who were committed to Eucharist to come together and do something we had never done before as a whole congregation: vote. The leadership team shared that we would require an 80 percent affirmation in order to purchase the building. We all filled out ballots, and while the 101 cards were counted in the other room, we Dalmatians nervously ate pizza.

Ten minutes later, one of the counters asked if she could announce the tally to the community. Out of 101 cards that came in, the vote was unanimous: we had 101 affirmations. One hundred percent agreement. The room freaked out! People were cheering and hugging and jumping up and down. The kids looked around, confused, and kept eating pizza. It was exciting to move ahead with the building, but it was way more than that: for the first time, we had discerned a united way forward together, and the vote was unanimous!

Forget everything else in this book: that's the real church miracle.

Like a Seed

The late, great Rachel Held Evans once said that "death is something empires worry about . . . not something resurrection people worry about."

The Romanian Baptist Church embodied this statement.

Hamilton was in a very different place than when we had moved downtown years earlier. The city had experienced a radical transformation: streets that were once barren were now littered with coffee shops and small boutique stores. The Romanian Baptist Church was just around the corner from Beasley Park, where I had fallen in love with Hamilton. No longer the third-poorest postal code in Canada, it was an economically diverse and flourishing neighborhood, albeit one whose housing market was becoming unsustainable. Most property in the neighborhood had doubled or tripled in value over just a few years. Our city had changed and, with it, so had the conversation about how to faithfully love, serve, and inhabit it. The Romanian Baptists could have sold their building to one of the many condo developers looking for their next project. The land alone was worth at least a million dollars. But they weren't looking for money, nor were they clinging to the glory days of their own congregation. They knew this was about more than *their* church. It was about *the* Church.

And she wasn't even close to done.

They told us they would sell us the building for less than half the price it was worth—for about as much as a house in the neighborhood. They were resurrection people, unafraid to die well, falling like a seed into the ground.

We also made a commitment to them that when our time was done, we would hand the building to another group of Jesus followers, ensuring it continued to be a place where God's kingdom met downtown Hamilton. We still don't know when it will be our time to die—it may be in a decade or perhaps a hundred years from now. But there will come a day when Eucharist will have to follow the example set before us. We will need to pass the baton on to the next generation, entrusting them with our insights, failures, and resources.

But this was not our day to die.

This was our time to receive the baton and step, once again, into the dangerous unknown.

Letters to the Church

Discerned and decided, there was just one small step between where we were and where God had called us: we needed money. Our church was able to carry the expenses of the space, and our scrappy attitude meant we had a small savings account to cover some of the closing costs. But it still wasn't enough. Just closing the deal and doing the initial repairs were going to cost us $100,000 more than what we had in the bank. We looked around the congregation and while, seven years in, there were a few people with financial resources, we didn't have the capacity to raise the difference within our own community.

We were going to need to ask the wider church if she could help us.

A videographer in our community made a short film about the building project, and some graphic designers created a fundraising brochure and web page. We posted our story online and prayed.

At first, it was just one email. "Congratulations, your charity has just received a donation of $50."

"Yes, it's working!" I yelled to Jill over my laptop. "Just two thousand more of those!" Then the donations began to pick up steam: $50 donations, followed by $200 donations, followed by $1,000 donations, followed by $20 donations. The little fundraising thermometer was filling up. But even more encouraging than the financial gifts were the cards and messages that accompanied them:

"We are so glad this community exists. We've been following you online for years and you give us hope for the future of the church."

"My daughter walked away from the faith feeling judged and shamed, but you've been a place where she can fully belong."

"We've been praying for you and we'll continue to pray for you. We need more churches like Eucharist."

The messages came in from parents and friends, those who loved Jesus, and neighbors who had never stepped into a church.

Congregations across the country wrote us into their budget, and businesses in downtown Hamilton donated to the cause. Behind each of these gifts and in every letter was the same message:

God called you all to church plant.

And you are totally supposed to exist.

A+.

By the end of the month, we had raised more than we needed.

It was official: we were buying a 125-year-old church building. But it wasn't the sort of building that was going to impress people. It was neither renowned and awe-inspiring nor modern and efficient. The stained-glass windows were literally falling apart, with plenty of cracks to let the light in. It was dirty and gritty but had a solid foundation. It had been beat up, but it was resilient.

It was us.

After the deal had been signed, but before we got the keys, Meg and I drove by the building during a magnificent snowstorm. We got out of the car and watched it through the static, slowly letting the severity of the situation wash over us.

Why in the world would we take on this project?

The slow work of restoration wouldn't be a smart investment. We'd never get our money back. Any other group would have knocked it down for the real estate. It was an old sanctuary right downtown, with no backyard or outdoor space, next to a busy four-lane road. The house next door had two couches in the front yard, a gutted car in the back, and an alleyway full of garbage and stray cats. The building had a leaky roof, there was absolutely no parking, and it was covered in graffiti.

Why would anyone do this?

Because it's worth it.

ACKNOWLEDGMENTS

During the writing of this book, my wife gave birth to our first child, and we were blessed to be supported by a team of midwives, friends, and family. In the same way, birthing this book was a team effort and, if I'm being perfectly honest, a lot harder than giving birth to our daughter.

For me! For me. My wife assures me that, despite being an artist, I'm not nearly as tortured as a woman in labor.

Okay, so, with that said, there are a few people to thank.

Thanks to my agent, Karen Neumair, and the team at Credo for guiding me and my anxieties through this process. To the incredible people at Baker Books, specifically my editor, Rachel Jacobson, and Kristin Adkinson, who is a grammar wizard. Thank you for putting up with my many questions and strong opinions and for giving me wise and gracious feedback that made this book better.

My deep gratitude to those who read this book at various times through the process, especially Brooks Reynolds, Patti Hall, and Kelly Bennet Heyd, who did edits of this book out of the goodness of their hearts. Hopefully, together; we've tricked readers into thinking I know how to properly use a semicolon.

To Pastor Bandula, Angel, and Tashia, as well as the Peiris and Fernando families, who helped make our two months in Sri Lanka possible. Without that time, I never would have completed the first draft of this book. We miss your beautiful country and Spirit-filled church. Thank you also to the Milnes for allowing me to take over your cottage for a final writing blitz. On the Hamilton front, thank you, Cannon, Mulberry, Work (RIP), and Synonym, for being my office away from the office.

Every morning, before writing, I'd be kicked in the teeth by Steven Pressfield and then inspired by the music of John Coltrane, as well as the soundtracks to *Celeste*, *Fez*, *Sword & Sworcery*, and *Pyre*. Thanks for helping me get into orbit.

To friends and mentors who cheered me on along the way and stopped our church from becoming a tire fire. I'm beyond grateful to the Witts for nine years of helping us not explode, the Friesens and Pernell for wisdom in the early days, and my fabulous copastor, Jill Trites. Please promise you'll never retire, because if you aren't working next to me, reminding me of the Good News and making inappropriate jokes, I will just shrivel up and die.

Thanks to all my good friends and group chats who keep me level, especially the Strangely Quiet Pals, the Pastors' Therapy Group, and the Original Five.

A special shout-out to TrueCity Hamilton, whose witness to church unity is more important than any single congregation. Eucharist would take a bullet for you.

To my family, who constantly remind me they are proud of me, even when I'm an idiot, and to my housemates, who kept cheering me on through late-night edit sessions.

Meg, you are the best person I have ever known, and I can't believe you love me.

Clem and Oscar, you are the anchors of my life and my greatest joy. I can't wait to see what you'll do when you're standing on our shoulders.

And finally, to the Eucharist Church community who, for nearly ten years, has been trying to incarnate the Good News in downtown Hamilton. There are easier churches to be a part of. Thanks for choosing to get your hands dirty together. I'm forever grateful to follow the way of Jesus with you.

NOTES

Prologue Why Would Anyone Do This?

11 "The truth is you could slit my throat, and . . . I'd apologize for bleeding on your shirt": "You're So Last Summer," MP3 audio, track 9 on Taking Back Sunday, *Tell All Your Friends*, Concord Bicycle Assets, 2002.

14 We had to live out the answers together, little by little, over a long period of time is a reference to this quote: "You have been given questions to which you cannot be *given* answers. You will have to live them out—perhaps a little at a time," from Wendell Berry, *Jayber Crow* (Berkeley, CA: Counterpoint, 2001), 54.

15 Organized religion has covered up sexual abuse scandals and participated in cultural genocide: One example of this "cultural genocide" in my own country is the residential school system. For more information about this, visit https://www.cbc.ca/news/canada/a-history-of-residential-schools-in-canada-1.702280.

16 About half of all the young people raised in American churches will walk away disillusioned: Neil Monahan and Saeed Ahmed, "There Are Now as Many Americans Who Claim No Religion as There Are Evangelicals and Catholics, a Survey Finds," CNN, April 26, 2019, https://www.cnn.com/2019/04/13/us/no-religion-largest-group-first-time-usa-trnd/index.html.

16 My country is on track to close over nine thousand sacred buildings in the next decade: Bonnie Allen, "From Sacred to Secular: Canada Set to Lose 9,000 Churches, Warns National Heritage Group," CBC, March 10, 2019, https://www.cbc.ca/news/canada/losing-churches-canada-1.5046812.

18 "The Word became flesh": John 1:14.

Chapter 1 Getting Our Hands Dirty

23 These party lines ran not only through our congregation but through our extended family as well: A few years ago, when my grandma was in her nineties, I asked her about this family divide and why she and Grandpa had chosen the Missouri Synod over the Evangelical Lutheran Church in Canada (ELCIC). She told me, "When we met, I was from the ELCIC and your grandfather was from

Missouri Synod. When we got married, we decided we would look and see which church was closer, and that would be our church. There was a Missouri Synod church right around the corner, so that's what we chose." To think, all that drama came out of such an arbitrary decision!

24 Jesus talks about the Good News being like seeds that are scattered: Mark 4:1–8.

24 Jesus also describes a farmer who goes to sleep: Mark 4:26–29.

24 Jesus asks his listeners to consider the mustard seed: Mark 4:30–32.

25 Noting that while he planted seeds and others watered, only God could make it grow: 1 Corinthians 3:3–9.

25 Who encountered the resurrected Jesus and mistook him for a gardener: John 20:11–18.

30 Even Jesus said that his disciples would do greater things than he had done: John 14:12.

Chapter 2 Falling into Place

32 Falling into Place is an expression borrowed from the title of friend and Hamilton poet John Terpstra's book of poetry (Kentville, NS: Gaspereau Press, 2002), which he describes in the subtitle as "what happens when one person becomes completely enamoured of the landscape in the city where he lives." It's absolutely recommended reading for any "place" lovers.

33 There are even stories of other nearby cities shipping their poor citizens to Hamilton: Graeme Smith, "Toronto's Homeless Program Stirs Resentment in Hamilton," *The Globe and Mail*, updated April 12, 2018, https://www.theglobe and mail.com/news/national/torontos-homeless-program-stirs-resentment-in -hamilton/article18416589/.

35 Israel's story begins with God calling a man named Abram to leave his father's land and go to a particular place: Genesis 12:1.

42 "No, I want you to go back to your neighborhood, find the poor, find your own Calcutta": "Mother Teresa Urged NY Nun to 'Find Your Own Calcutta,'" WRAL. com, September 2, 2016, https://www.wral.com/mother-teresa-urged-ny-nun-to -find-your-own-calcutta-/15982746/.

Chapter 3 The "Right" Way to Start a Church

45 After a day filled with miracles, including the soon-to-be-famous "feeding of the five thousand," Jesus sends the disciples across the lake by boat: This chapter focuses on and paraphrases a story told in Matthew 14:13–34.

48 Faith leaders have observed that no church is neutral in terms of its culture: One of the earliest people to note our blindness to our own culture was missionary Lesslie Newbigin.

48 "Culturally commuting": The simplest exploration of what this blindness to our culture looks like in young, urban congregations is probably from Nadia Bolz-Weber, who uses the phrase *culturally commute* to talk about certain people joining the church. The first reference I could find to her using it was in an article for

Sojourners: "My Definition of the Emerging Church," March 23, 2009, https://sojo.net/articles/my-definition-emerging-church.

Chapter 4 Faith Is Communal

60 **When the word gets out that Jesus is back in town, the entire region comes to see him:** This paraphrased account comes from Luke 5:17–20.

62 **A Roman centurion has enough faith to heal—not himself but his servant:** Luke 7:1–10.

62 **A woman has faith to heal her daughter:** Mark 7:25–30.

62 **Being friends as an adult is just saying, "'We should really hang out more' over and over again until one of you dies":** Lyndsey Gallant (@apocalynds), Twitter post, https://twitter.com/apocalynds/status/889169062047174658?lang=en.

Chapter 5 The Night the Children Never Came

70 **Five thousand men come to see Jesus with their families in tow:** This paraphrased account comes from Matthew 14:13–21.

74 **The same God who rained bread down from heaven for the Israelites and sent ravens to deliver food to the prophets:** See Exodus 16:1–5 and 1 Kings 17:2–6.

Chapter 6 Nap Sunday

79 **The writer of the book of Hebrews compares our life on earth to running with endurance the race that is marked before us:** Author's paraphrase of Hebrews 12:1.

83 **You can't sell "Remember, You're Going to Die" cards:** The very funny Nadia Bolz-Weber was the first person I read who joked about the absurd idea of selling products for Ash Wednesday: "Why I Love Lent: Sin Is One of My Favorite Things to Talk About," *Sarcastic Lutheran*, February 22, 2012, https://www.patheos.com/blogs/nadiabolzweber/2012/02/why-i-love-ash-wednesday-and-lent-part-1-sin/.

84 **We "play and pray":** According to an article in the *Christian Post*, Eugene Peterson used this language in a discussion at the Q Ideas Conference: Clare Morris, "Eugene Peterson: Celebration of the Sabbath Provides Opportunity for God to Act," *Christian Post*, February 28, 2012, https://www.christianpost.com/news/eugene-peterson-celebration-of-the-sabbath-provides-opportunity-for-god-to-act.html.

85 **"Unforced rhythms of grace"** is a quote from Eugene Peterson's translation of Matthew 11:28–30 in *The Message*. Yes, I realize that's two Peterson references in a row, but I could spend this whole chapter just quoting him. Seriously, his books *The Pastor* (New York: HarperCollins, 2012) and *Under the Unpredictable Plant* (Grand Rapids, MI: Eerdmans, 1994) were read annually by me during the early years of Eucharist. If I were to summon a Patronus, it would just be Eugene Peterson hopping around.

87 **"The sabbath was made for humankind, and not humankind for the sabbath":** Mark 2:27.

88 **"Therefore I tell you, do not worry about your life, what you will eat or what you will drink":** Matthew 6:25.

Chapter 7 The Kingdom of God Is Like a Potluck

93 How do we stick together when we're all so different?: I have actually written about this far more thoroughly in a short e-book called *How We Believe: Unity, Diversity, and the 123's of Theology*. You can find it by visiting my website, www .kevinmakins.com.

94 The Bible describes God's mission as the reconciliation of all things, a master plan to bring every fractured piece of creation back together again: Colossians 1:20 and 2 Corinthians 5:18–20 illustrate how this is God's vision for humanity. Ephesians 2:11–22 explores how the church becomes the place where these different groups are reconciled in Christ's body and around his table.

95 "There is no longer Jew or Greek, there is no longer slave or free, there is no longer male and female; for all of you are one in Christ Jesus": Galatians 3:28.

99 But following that moment of bliss is the realization that you have to pay for the meal, which doesn't feel so good now that you're no longer hungry: Jerry Seinfeld has a great bit about this on *Seinfeld*, season 1, episode 4, "The Stock Tip."

Chapter 8 The Most Honest Place in Town

106 "Church of the Young and Hip": Amy Kenny, *Hamilton Spectator*, August 10, 2013, https://www.thespec.com/news-story/4026981-church-of-the-young-and-hip/.

107 Experts believe that in our digital world, the average person sees up to ten thousand advertisements a day: Jon Simpson, "Finding Brand Success In The Digital World," *Forbes*, August 25, 2017, https://www.forbes.com/sites/forbesagency council/2017/08/25/finding-brand-success-in-the-digital-world/#37de30f1626e.

108 "Darkness is my closest friend": Psalm 88:18 (NIV).

109 "Churches should be the most honest place in town, not the happiest place in town": Brueggemann is quoted in Peter Enns, "When God Is Unfaithful," Patheos, October 24, 2013, https://www.patheos.com/blogs/peterenns/2013/10/when-god -is-unfaithful/.

Chapter 9 A Particular Glory

117 The cloud of God's glory overwhelms the room, and all the people fall flat on their faces in fear and reverence: 1 Kings 8:6–14.

118 One of the nations they buddy up with, Babylon, eventually turns on Israel: 2 Kings 25.

118 As the dark smoke of the burning temple vanishes into the air, so does the glory of God: To learn more about the Babylonian judgment and how it shapes the biblical story, I recommend reading Craig G. Bartholomew and Michael W. Goheen, *The Drama of Scripture* (Grand Rapids, MI: Baker Academic, 2014), or watching videos by The Bible Project on YouTube. Start with their video "The Way of the Exile" (https://www.youtube.com/watch?v=XzWpa0gcPyo), and then just watch all of them over and over.

118 Never underestimate the impact of a good coffee shop: In this case, the coffee shop in question is The Cannon in lower-city Hamilton, Ontario, Canada. If you're ever in Hamilton, you must go to The Cannon and get their waffle sandwiches.

120 **They follow him in the stillness of night, through the camp and toward the base of a nearby mountain, where he begins his ascent:** This story is found in Matthew 17, but after this chapter you should also listen to the song "The Transfiguration" by Sufjan Stevens (MP3 audio, track 12 on *Seven Swans*, Asthmatic Kitty, 2004), just to get in the mood.

124 **"I think it is right to refresh your memory as long as I live in *the tent of this body*":** 2 Peter 1:13 (NIV; emphasis mine).

126 **"A vinegar we are pickled into for life":** In Leshia's sermon, I learned that Martin Luther, my childhood popstar, had once said that if ever provoked by the devil, we should yell at him, "Away from me, Satan, I am baptized." Not I *was* baptized. I *am* baptized. Our baptism isn't a washing away of dirt, but a submersion into God's holy vinegar.

126 **To them, it wasn't a question of *if* but *when* Eucharist would rip herself to pieces:** Shortly after finishing this chapter, I read Richard Rohr's book *The Universal Christ* (New York: Convergent, 2019), which gets into the themes of this chapter with more clarity and more Franciscan charm than I could. There is plenty in the book worth wrestling and even disagreeing with. The chapter "Things at Their Depth" seems to particularly dovetail with this chapter's themes of particularity and universality.

Chapter 10 New Church

129 **All he wants is one last meal with his disciples:** You can read about this final meal in John 13.

130 **"To love at all is to be vulnerable":** C. S. Lewis, *The Four Loves* (New York: Harcourt Brace, 1960), 121. "To love at all is to be vulnerable. Love anything, and your heart will certainly be wrung and possibly be broken. If you want to make sure of keeping it intact, you must give your heart to no one, not even to an animal. Wrap it carefully round with hobbies and little luxuries; avoid all entanglements; lock it up safe in the casket or coffin of your selfishness. But in that casket—safe, dark, motionless, airless—it will change. It will not be broken; it will become unbreakable, impenetrable, irredeemable."

132 **After the arrest, Peter and another disciple head to the courtyard of the high priest, where Jesus is being held:** This paraphrased account comes from John 18:15–27.

135 **Spoiler alert: Jesus doesn't stay dead:** This paraphrased account comes from John 20–21.

136 **Sometimes I think her job is to professionally push me out of my comfort zone:** Jill recently released a book, *Even the Sparrow* (Grand Rapids, MI: Kregel, 2019), about her time as a prayer missionary in Hamilton, and if you read it, you'll learn she's every bit as wonderful and challenging as I implied.

139 **Only forgiveness can suck the toxin out of us:** To be clear, forgiveness isn't the same thing as reconciliation. To reconcile is to reconnect the relationship (to reenter the marriage or friendship), but to forgive someone is to release our grip on them and hand them over to God. It's to trust that God is more capable of sorting out the situation than you or I could ever be, so we no longer need to try to control things, and we no longer need to cling to our hurt.

Chapter 12 Everything We're Not

157 **The human body is made up of many different parts, but each part works for the good of the whole:** Paul's reflections on the church as a body can be found in 1 Corinthians 12:12–31.

159 **"The eye cannot say to the hand, 'I have no need of you'":** 1 Corinthians 12:21.

160 **Start as small and near as possible:** In his last interview ever, which was with Jonathan Merritt, Eugene Peterson gave some great practical advice about finding a church:

> Go to the nearest smallest church and commit yourself to being there for 6 months. If it doesn't work out, find somewhere else. But don't look for programs, don't look for entertainment, and don't look for a great preacher. A Christian congregation is not a glamorous place, not a romantic place. That's what I always told people. If people were leaving my congregation to go to another place of work, I'd say, "The smallest church, the closest church, and *stay there* for 6 months." Sometimes it doesn't work. Some pastors are just incompetent. And some are flat out bad. So I don't think that's the answer to everything, but it's a better place to start than going to the one with all the programs, the glitz, all that stuff.

"Faithful to the End: An Interview with Eugene Peterson," Religion News Service, September 27, 2013, https://religionnews.com/2013/09/27/faithful-end-in terview-eugene-peterson/.

161 **"Everything I'm not made me everything I am":** "Everything I Am," featuring DJ Premier, MP3 audio, track 10 on *Graduation*, Roc-A-Fella, 2007.

Chapter 13 Dying Well

164 **The early church started with a bang:** The summary I give in this section is a reference to Acts 2–6.

171 **"Death is something empires worry about . . . not something resurrection people worry about":** Rachel Held Evans, *Searching for Sunday* (Nashville: Nelson Books, 2015), 225. Thank you, Rachel, for your words and your courage. Your fingerprints are on the heart of our community and so many congregations like ours.

Kevin Makins (MDiv, Heritage Seminary) is the founding pastor of Eucharist Church in downtown Hamilton, Ontario, in Canada, which has been recognized as one of the most creative and innovative churches in the country and spotlighted on national television and radio outlets, in newspapers, and on podcasts. A frequent speaker at conferences and churches, Kevin also performs one-man shows in bars and makes videos for thousands on YouTube. His audience includes the faithful and the skeptical, those hungry to learn, and those who just want to hear a good story. He lives in an old house downtown with his wife, kids, and housemates.

CONNECT WITH KEVIN

kevinmakins.com

 kevinmakins

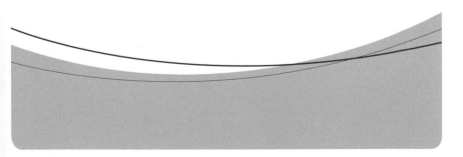

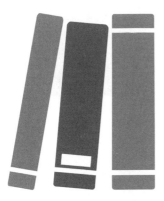

LIKE THIS
BOOK?
Consider sharing it with others!

This is my first book, which means you are like one of those cool kids who is into an indie band long before anyone else knows about them. Congratulations. It also means I need your help to get this book into the hands of others who will appreciate it.

There are plenty of creative ways to get the word out, but here are a few simple options:

- Buy a copy for someone with whom you think the message of this book will resonate. Many of the books I love most were gifts from friends who knew me.

- Start a book club in your church or small group, and allow each chapter of this book to set the tone for your conversation.

- Write a book review on Goodreads, Amazon, or your blog or social media feed. These truly go a long way toward helping people know the book is worth reading.

- Post about the book on Twitter, Facebook, Instagram, or TikTok if you're feeling really creative. Use the hashtag **#WhyWouldAnyoneGoToChurch**

- If you're not sure what to write, I suggest this:
  "I loved **#WhyWouldAnyoneGoToChurch** by @kevinmakins, and he seems very cool and popular." Actually, that might get weird. Just write something genuine!

- Follow Baker Books on social media, tell them what you liked about the book, and pay attention to their new releases because they've got really good taste.

Thank you so much for reading this book to the final page, and a special thank you to anyone who helps get the book into the hands of others. Grace and peace.

E